# The Gulf Coast

*Other Books in This Series:*

The California Coast
The Great Lakes
The Great North American Prairie
The North Atlantic Coast
The South Atlantic Coast and Piedmont

## The *Stories from Where We Live* Series

Each volume in the *Stories from Where We Live* series celebrates a North American ecoregion through its own distinctive literature. For thousands of years, people have told stories to convey their community's cultural and natural history. *Stories from Where We Live* reinvigorates that tradition in hopes of helping young people better understand the place where they live. The anthologies feature poems, stories, and essays from historical and contemporary authors, as well as from the oral traditions of each region's indigenous peoples. Together they document the geographic richness of the continent and reflect the myriad ways that people interact with and respond to the natural world. We hope that these stories kindle readers' imaginations and inspire them to explore, observe, ponder, and protect the place they call home.

Please visit www.milkweed.org for a teaching guide to this book and more information on the *Stories from Where We Live* series.

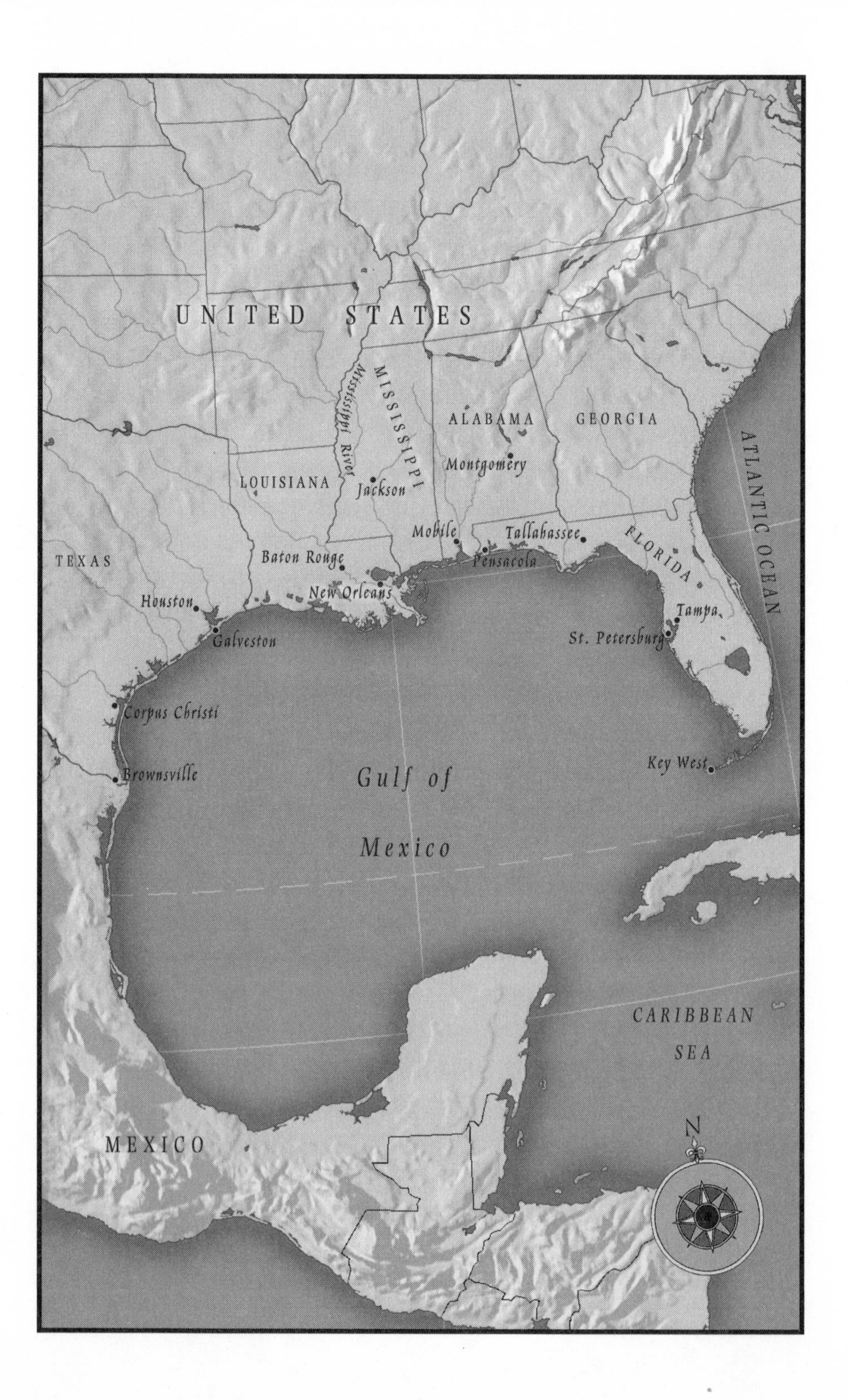
UNITED STATES
MISSISSIPPI
Mississippi River
ALABAMA
GEORGIA
ATLANTIC OCEAN
Montgomery
LOUISIANA
Jackson
Mobile
Tallahassee
FLORIDA
TEXAS
Baton Rouge
Pensacola
New Orleans
Houston
Tampa
Galveston
St. Petersburg
Corpus Christi
Brownsville
Key West
Gulf of
Mexico
CARIBBEAN
SEA
MEXICO
N

# The Gulf Coast

## Stories from Where We Live

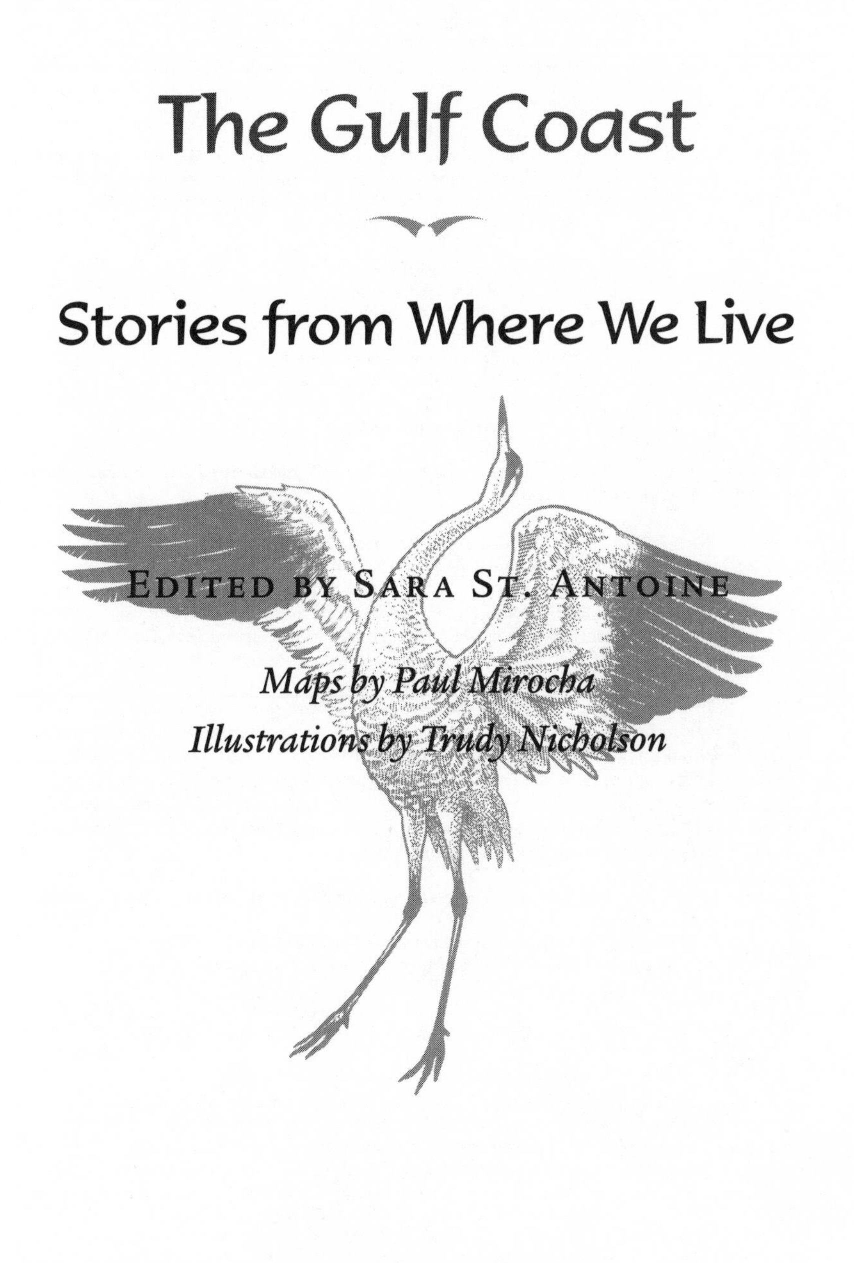

EDITED BY SARA ST. ANTOINE

*Maps by Paul Mirocha*

*Illustrations by Trudy Nicholson*

MILKWEED EDITIONS

Published 2006 by Milkweed Editions
Printed in Canada
Illustrations by Trudy Nicholson
Maps by Paul Mirocha
Interior design by Wendy Holdman
The text of this book is set in Legacy.
06 07 08 09 10 5 4 3 2 1
*First Paperback Edition*

Milkweed Editions, a nonprofit publisher, specially thanks Joe B. and Harriet Foster for their generous underwriting support of this book.

Milkweed Editions, a nonprofit publisher, gratefully acknowledges sustaining support from Emilie and Henry Buchwald; Bush Foundation; Patrick and Aimee Butler Family Foundation; Cargill Value Investment; Timothy and Tara Clark Family Charitable Fund; Dougherty Family Foundation; Ecolab Foundation; General Mills Foundation; John and Joanne Gordon; Greystone Foundation; Institute for Scholarship in the Liberal Arts, College of Arts and Sciences, University of Notre Dame; Constance B. Kunin; Marshall BankFirst; Marshall Field's Gives; May Department Stores Company Foundation; McKnight Foundation; a grant from the Minnesota State Arts Board, through an appropriation by the Minnesota State Legislature, a grant from the National Endowment for the Arts, and private funders; an award from the National Endowment for the Arts, which believes that a great nation deserves great art; Navarre Corporation; Debbie Reynolds; St. Paul Travelers Foundation; Ellen and Sheldon Sturgis; Target Foundation; Gertrude Sexton Thompson Charitable Trust (George R. A. Johnson, Trustee); James R. Thorpe Foundation; Toro Foundation; Serene and Christopher Warren; W. M. Foundation; and Xcel Energy Foundation.

Library of Congress Cataloging-in-Publication Data

Stories from where we live. The Gulf Coast
The Gulf Coast / edited by Sara St. Antoine ; maps by Paul Mirocha ; illustrations by Trudy Nicholson. — 1st ed.
p. cm. — (Stories from where we live)
Originally published: Stories from where we live. The Gulf Coast. 2002.
Includes index.
ISBN-13: 978-1-57131-665-3 (pbk. : alk. paper)
ISBN-10: 1-57131-665-5 (pbk. : alk. paper)
1. Gulf Coast (U.S.)—Miscellanea—Juvenile literature. 2. Gulf Coast (U.S.)—Biography—Juvenile literature. 3. Natural history—Gulf Coast (U.S.)—Miscellanea—Juvenile literature. 4. Gulf Coast (U.S.)—Literary collections. 5. American literature—Gulf Coast (U.S.) I. St. Antoine, Sara, 1966- II. Mirocha, Paul. III. Nicholson, Trudy H. IV. Title. V. Series.
F296.S76 2006
976—dc22

2006016650

This book is printed on acid-free paper.

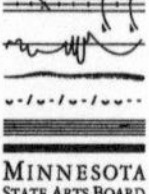

## The Gulf Coast

## Wild Lives

## Appendixes: Ecology of the Gulf Coast

# An Invitation

Wander along the bayous and byways of the Gulf Coast and you can hear the cries of gulls mingling with the voices of shrimpers heading out for a day at sea. You can hear frogs trilling and croaking in a secluded stretch of swamp, and musicians cranking out zydeco or jazz in packed music halls. And wherever you go in this coastal region, you're bound to hear stories. Fishing tales. Cajun animal stories. Choctaw legends. Songs from the cotton fields.

The Gulf Coast is a region of storytellers. And if you listen closely to them, you'll hear more than just riveting narratives. Like storytellers everywhere, those in the Gulf Coast fill their tales with information and reflections on the world around them. Some stories offer us a glimpse of historical events and famous people. Some portray the cultural traditions of a community. And many, including those we've gathered in this anthology, tell us about a region's unique plants, animals, and natural places, and the ways they sustain and enrich the lives of local people.

The Gulf Coast region as we've defined it is a huge arc of land that surrounds the Gulf of Mexico. It stretches from the beaches and bottomland forests of east Texas to the bayous and floodplain forests of Louisiana and Mississippi to the swamps, islands, and seashores of Alabama and Florida, including the Florida Keys. Some of the region lies well inland from the salty Gulf. But all of it is characterized by a mild and humid climate, low-lying and often waterlogged lands, and a wondrous profusion of life.

In this anthology, you'll discover some of the many sides of the Gulf Coast region. In "Adventures" you'll read about the sweet delights of scalloping and the sure terrors of hurricanes and floods. In "Great Places" you'll journey across sandy beaches, cypress swamps, backyards, and bayous. In "Reapers and Sowers" you'll meet some of the many people who rely on and cultivate the natural resources of the region, from cotton farmers to hunters to berry pickers. And in "Wild Lives" you'll encounter a colorful menagerie of wild creatures, including alligators, egrets, rattlesnakes, manatees, and mosquitoes.

We're sure you'll relish the lively and often humor-filled accounts that fill this anthology. And we hope they'll inspire you to take a closer look at the natural wonders of the Gulf Coast ecoregion or whatever place you call home.

—Sara St. Antoine

# The Gulf Coast

# Adventures

# A Creature in the Bay of St. Louis

BARRY HANNAH

*When people cast a line into the waters of the Gulf of Mexico, they hope they'll wind up with a big fish. But sometimes they also come home with a great story.*

We were out early in the brown water, the light still gray and wet.

My cousin Woody and I were wading on an oyster shell reef in the bay. We had cheap bait-casting rods and reels with black cotton line, at the end of which were a small bell weight and a croaker hook. We used peeled shrimp for bait. Sometimes you might get a speckled trout or flounder, but more likely you would catch the croaker. A large one weighed a half pound. When caught and pulled in the fish made a metallic croaking sound. It is one of the rare fish who talk to you about their plight when they are landed. My aunt fried them crispy, covered in cornmeal, and they were delicious, especially with lemon juice and ketchup.

A good place to fish was near the pilings of the Saint Stanislaus school pier. The pier gate was locked but you could wade to the pilings and the oyster shell reef. Up the bluff above us on the town road was a fish market and the Star Theater, where we saw movies.

Many cats, soft and friendly and plump, would gather

around the edges of the fish market and when you went to the movies you would walk past three or four of them who would ease against your leg as if asking to go to the movie with you. The cats were very social. In their prosperity they seemed to have organized into a watching society of leisure and culture. Nobody yelled at them because this was a very small coastal town where everybody knew each other. Italians, Slavs, French, Negroes, Methodists, Baptists, and Catholics. You did not want to insult the cat's owner by rudeness. Some of the cats would tire of the market offerings and come down the bluff to watch you fish, patiently waiting for their share of your take or hunting the edges of the weak surf for dead crabs and fish. You would be pulling in your fish, catch it, and when you looked ashore the cats were suddenly alert. They were wise. It took a hard case not to leave them one good fish for supper.

That night as you went into an Abbott and Costello movie, which cost a dime, that same cat you had fed might rub against your leg and you felt sorry it couldn't go into the movie house with you. You might be feeling comical when you came out and saw the same cat waiting with conviction as if there were something in there it wanted very much, and you threw a Jujube down to it on the sidewalk. A Jujube was a pellet of chewing candy the quality of vulcanized rubber. You chewed several during the movie and you had a wonderful syrup of licorice, strawberry, and lime in your mouth. But the cat would look down at the Jujube, then up at you as if you were insane, and you felt badly for betraying this serious creature and hated that you were mean and thoughtless. That is the kind of conscience you had in Bay St. Louis, Mississippi, where you were always close to folks and creatures.

This morning we had already had a good trip as the sun

began coming out. The croakers swam in a burlap sack tied to a piling and underwater. The sacks were free at the grocery, and people called them croaker sacks. When you lifted the sack to put another croaker in you heard that froggy metal noise in a chorus, quite loud, and you saw the cats on shore hearken to it too. We would have them with french-fried potatoes, fat tomato slices from my uncle's garden, and a large piece of deep sweet watermelon for supper.

It made a young boy feel good having the weight of all these fish in the dripping sack when you lifted it, knowing you had provided for a large family and maybe even neighbors at supper. You felt to be a small hero of some distinction, and ahead of you was that mile walk through the neighborhood lanes where adults would pay attention to your catch and salute you. The fishing rod on your shoulder, you had done some solid bartering with the sea; you were not to be trifled with.

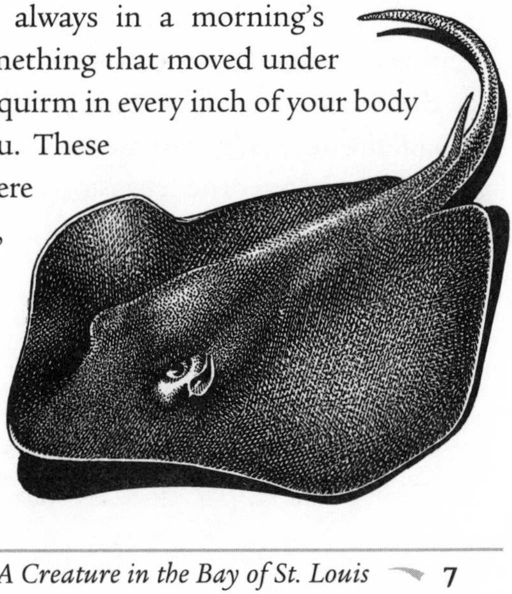

The only dangerous thing in the bay was a stingaree, with its poisonous barbed hook of a tail. This ray would lie flat, covered over by sand like a flounder. We waded barefoot in swimming trunks and almost always in a morning's fishing you stepped on something that moved under your foot and you felt the squirm in every inch of your body before it got off from you. These could be stingarees. There were terrible legends about them, always a story from summers ago when a stingaree had whipped its tail into the calf of some unfortunate girl or boy and buried the vile hook deep in the flesh. The child came dragging out of the water with this twenty-pound brownish black monster the size of a garbage can lid attached to his leg, thrashing and sucking with its awful mouth. Then the child's leg grew black and swelled hugely and they had to amputate it, and that child was in the attic of some dark house on the edge of town, never the same again and pale like a thing that never saw light; then eventually the child turned into half-stingaree and they took it away to an institution for special cases. So you believed all this most positively and when a being squirmed under your foot you were likely to walk on water out of there. We should never forget that when frightened a child can fly short distances too.

The high tide was receding with the sun clear up and smoking in the east over Biloxi, the sky reddening, and the croakers were not biting so well anymore. But each new fish would give more pride to the sack and I was greedy for a few more since I didn't get to fish in salt water much. I lived four hours north in a big house with a clean lawn, a maid, and yardmen, but it was landlocked and grim when you compared it to this place of my cousin's. Much later I learned his family was nearly poor, but this was laughable even when I heard it, because it was heaven: the movie house right where you fished and the society of cats, and my uncle's house with the huge watermelons lying on the linoleum under the television with startling shows like *Lights Out!* from the New Orleans station. We didn't even have a television station yet where I lived.

I kept casting and wading out deeper toward an old creosoted pole in the water where I thought a much bigger croaker or even a flounder might be waiting. My cousin was tired and red-burnt from yesterday in the sun, so he went to swim under the diving board of the Catholic high school a hundred yards away. They had dredged a pool. Otherwise the sea was very shallow a long ways out. But now I was almost up to my chest, near the barnacled pole where a big boat could tie up. I kept casting and casting, almost praying toward the deep water around the pole for a big fish. The lead and shrimp would plunk and tumble into a dark hole, I thought, where a special giant fish was lurking, something too big for the croaker shallows.

My grandmother had caught a seven-pound flounder from the seawall years ago and she was still honored for it, my uncle retelling the tale about her whooping out, afraid but happy, the pole bent double. I wanted to have a story like that about me. The fish made Mama Hannah so happy, my older cousin said, that he saw her dancing to a band on television by herself when everybody else was asleep. Soon—I couldn't bear to think about it—in a couple of days they would drive me over to Gulfport and put me on a bus for home, and in my sorrow there waited a dry red brick school within bitter tasting distance. But even that would be sweetened by a great fish and its story.

It took place in no more than half a minute, I'd guess, but it had the lengthy rapture and terror of a whole tale. Something bit and then was jerking, small but solidly, then it was too big, and I began moving in the water and grabbing the butt of the rod again because what was on had taken it out of my hands. When I caught the rod up, I was moving toward the barnacled pole with the tide slopping on it, and that was the only noise around. I went in to my neck in a muddier scoop in the bottom, and then under my feet something moved. I knew it was a giant stingaree instantly. Hard skin on a squirming plate of flesh. I was sorely terrified but was pulled even past this and could do nothing, now up to my chin and the stiff little pole bent violently double. I was dragged through the mud and I knew the being when it surfaced would be bigger than me and with much more muscle. Then, like something under water since Europe, seven or eight huge porpoises surfaced, blowing water in a loud group explosion out of their enormous heads, and I was just shot all over with light and nerves because they were only twenty feet from me and I connected them, the ray, and what was on my hook into a horrible combination beast that children who waded too far would be dragged out by and crushed and drowned.

The thing pulled with heavier tugs like a truck going up its gears. The water suddenly rushed into my face and into my nose. I could see only brown with the bottom of the sun shining through it.

I was gone, gone, and I thought of the cats watching onshore and said good-bye cat friends, good-bye Cousin Woody, good-bye young life, I am only a little boy and I'm not letting go of this pole, it is not even mine, it's my uncle's. Good-bye school, good-bye Mother and Daddy, don't weep for me, it is a thing in the water cave of my destiny. Yes, I thought all these things in detail while drowning and being pulled rushing through the water, but the sand came up under my feet and the line went slack; the end of the rod was broken off and hanging on the line. When I cranked in the line I saw the hook, a thick silver one, was straightened. The vacancy in the air where there was no fish was an awful thing, like surgery in the pit of my stomach. I convinced myself that I had almost had him.

When I stood in the water on solid sand, I began crying. I tried to stop but when I got close to Woody I burst out again.

He wanted to know what happened but I did not tell him the truth. Instead I told him I had stepped on an enormous ray and its hook had sliced me.

No.

Yes. I went into briefer sobs.

When we checked my legs there was a slice from an oyster shell, a fairly deep one I'd gotten while being pulled by the creature. I refused treatment and I was respected for my close call the rest of the day. I even worked in the lie more and said furthermore it didn't much matter to me if I was taken off to the asylum for stingaree children, that was just the breaks. My cousin and the rest of them looked at me anew and with concern but I was acting funny and they must have been baffled.

It wasn't until I was back in the dreaded schoolroom that I could even talk about the fish, and then my teacher doubted it, and she in goodwill with a smile told my father, congratulating me on my imagination. My father thought that was rich, but then I told him the same story, the creature so heavy like a truck, the school of porpoises, and he said That's enough. You didn't mention this when you came back.

No, and neither did I mention the two cats when I walked back to shore with Woody and the broken rod. They had watched all the time, and I knew it, because the both of them stared at me with big solemn eyes, a lot of light in them, and it was with the beings of fur then that I entrusted my confidences, and they knew I would be back to catch the big one, the singular monster, on that line going tight into the cave in the water, something thrashing on the end, celebrated above by porpoises.

I never knew what kind of fish it was, but I would return

and return to it the rest of my life, and the cats would be waiting to witness me and share my honor.

**Barry Hannah** *was born in Meridian, Mississippi. A former writer-in-residence at many colleges, including Clemson University, Middlebury College, and the University of Iowa, he now teaches at the University of Mississippi.*

# The Midnight Marsh

Kelly King Alexander

We glide into the quiet night
Like egrets, the moon reflecting our white flight
On the black water of the bayou.
Our pirogue swims like an alligator
Skimming the surface
And slaloming with ease
Around cypress knees and tupelo gum trees,
Festooned with Spanish moss
Shimmering silver in nature's nightlight.
An owl speaks
And I wonder, too,
Who burrows into bedcovers like crawfish in mud mounds?
Who buries his head in slumber, deaf to swamp sounds,
While life in the midnight marsh abounds?
Who?
Who?
Who?

**Kelly King Alexander** *has published her writing in many national magazines, including* Parents, Family Circle, Southern Living, *and* Cricket. *She lives with her husband, Lathan Alexander, and their children, Rachel, Alise, and Ethan, in the shade of several two-hundred-year-old live oaks on the banks of Bayou Manchac in Prairieville, Louisiana.*

# The Flood

## Zora Neale Hurston

*No Gulf Coast resident is immune from the devastating effects of a tropical hurricane. But in this excerpt from her novel* Their Eyes Were Watching God, *Zora Neale Hurston reveals how responding appropriately to an approaching hurricane depends in part one's depth of experience and sharpness of instinct. When the excerpt opens, Janie and her husband, Tea Cake, are living in the Florida Everglades, just south of Lake Okeechobee. They're part of a community of migrant farm workers made up of African Americans and immigrants from the Bahamas known as the "Saws."*

Since Tea Cake and Janie had friended with the Bahaman workers in the 'Glades, they, the "Saws," had been gradually drawn into the American crowd. They quit hiding out to hold their dances when they found that their American friends didn't laugh at them as they feared. Many of the Americans learned to jump and liked it as much as the "Saws." So they began to hold dances night after night in the quarters, usually behind Tea Cake's house. Often now, Tea Cake and Janie stayed up so late at the fire dances that Tea Cake would not let her go with him to the field. He wanted her to get her rest.

So she was home by herself one afternoon when she saw a band of Seminoles passing by. The men walking in front and the laden, stolid women following them like burros. She had seen Indians several times in the 'Glades, in twos and threes, but this was a large party. They were headed towards the Palm Beach road and kept moving steadily. About an hour later another party appeared and went the same way. Then another just before sundown. This time she asked where they were all going and at last one of the men answered her.

"Going to high ground. Saw-grass bloom. Hurricane coming."

Everybody was talking about it that night. But nobody was worried. The fire dance kept up till nearly dawn. The next day, more Indians moved east, unhurried but steady. Still a blue sky and fair weather. Beans running fine and prices good, so the Indians could be, *must* be, wrong. You couldn't have a hurricane when you're making seven and eight dollars a day picking beans. Indians are dumb anyhow, always were. Another night of Stew Beef making dynamic subtleties with his drum and living, sculptural, grotesques in the dance. Next day, no Indians passed at all. It was hot and sultry and Janie left the field and went home.

Morning came without motion. The winds, to the tiniest, lisping baby breath had left the earth. Even before the sun gave light, dead day was creeping from bush to bush watching man.

Some rabbits scurried through the quarters going east. Some possums slunk by and their route was definite. One or two at a time, then more. By the time the people left the fields the procession was constant. Snakes, rattlesnakes began to cross the quarters. The men killed a few, but they could not be missed from the crawling horde. People stayed indoors until daylight. Several times during the night Janie heard the snort of big animals like deer. Once the muted voice of a panther.

Going east and east. That night the palm and banana trees began that long distance talk with rain. Several people took fright and picked up and went in to Palm Beach anyway. A thousand buzzards held a flying meet and then went above the clouds and stayed.

One of the Bahaman boys stopped by Tea Cake's house in a car and hollered. Tea Cake came out throwin' laughter over his shoulder into the house.

"Hello Tea Cake."

"Hello 'Lias. You leavin', Ah see."

"Yeah man. You and Janie wanta go? Ah wouldn't give nobody else uh chawnce at uh seat till Ah found out if you all had anyway tuh go."

"Thank yuh ever so much, Lias. But we 'bout decided tuh stay."

"De crow gahn up, man."

"Dat ain't nothin'. You ain't seen de bossman go up, is yuh? Well all right now. Man, de money's too good on the muck. It's liable tuh fair off by tuhmorrer. Ah wouldn't leave if Ah wuz you."

"Mah uncle come for me. He say hurricane warning out in Palm Beach. Not so bad dere, but man, dis muck is too low and dat big lake is liable tuh bust."

"Ah naw, man. Some boys in dere now talkin' 'bout it. Some of 'em been in de 'Glades fuh years. 'Tain't nothin' but uh lil blow. You'll lose de whole day tuhmorrer tryin' tuh git back out heah."

"De Indians gahn east, man. It's dangerous."

"Dey don't always know. Indians don't know much uh nothin', tuh tell de truth. Else dey'd own dis country still. De white folks ain't gone nowhere. Dey oughta know if it's dangerous. You better stay heah, man. Big jumpin' dance tuhnight right heah, when it fair off."

Lias hesitated and started to climb out, but his uncle wouldn't let him. "Dis time tuhmorrer you gointuh wish you follow crow," he snorted and drove off. Lias waved back to them gaily.

"If Ah never see you no mo' on earth, Ah'll meet you in Africa."

Others hurried east like the Indians and rabbits and snakes

and coons. But the majority sat around laughing and waiting for the sun to get friendly again.

Several men collected at Tea Cake's house and sat around stuffing courage into each other's ears. Janie baked a big pan of beans and something she called sweet biscuits and they all managed to be happy enough. . . .

. . . Then they got to playing Florida flip and coon-can. Then it was dice. Not for money. This was a show-off game. Everybody posing his fancy shots. As always it broiled down to Tea Cake and Motor Boat. Tea Cake with his shy grin and Motor Boat with his face like a little black cherubim just from a church tower doing amazing things with anybody's dice. The others forgot the work and the weather watching them throw. It was art. A thousand dollars a throw in Madison Square Garden wouldn't have gotten any more breathless suspense. It would have just been more people holding in.

After a while somebody looked out and said, "It ain't gitting no fairer out dere. B'lieve Ah'll git on over tuh mah shack." Motor Boat and Tea Cake were still playing so everybody left them at it.

Sometime that night the winds came back. Everything in the world had a strong rattle, sharp and short like Stew Beef vibrating the drum head near the edge with his fingers. By morning Gabriel was playing the deep tones in the center of the drum. So when Janie looked out of her door she saw the drifting mists gathered in the west—that cloud field of the sky—to arm themselves with thunders and march forth against the world. Louder and higher and lower and wider the sound and motion spread, mounting, sinking, darking.

It woke up old Okechobee and the monster began to roll

in his bed. Began to roll and complain like a peevish world on a grumble. The folks in the quarters and the people in the big houses further around the shore heard the big lake and wondered. The people felt uncomfortable but safe because there were the seawalls to chain the senseless monster in his bed. The folks let the people do the thinking. If the castles thought themselves secure, the cabins needn't worry. Their decision was already made as always. Chink up your cracks, shiver in your wet beds and wait on the mercy of the Lord. The bossman might have the thing stopped before morning anyway. It is so easy to be hopeful in the day time when you can see the things you wish on. But it was night, it stayed night. Night was striding across nothingness with the whole round world in his hands.

A big burst of thunder and lightning that trampled over the roof of the house. So Tea Cake and Motor stopped playing. Motor looked up in his angel-looking way and said, "Big Massa draw him chair upstairs."

"Ah'm glad y'all stop dat crap-shootin' even if it wasn't for money," Janie said. "Ole Massa is doin' *His* work now. Us oughta keep quiet."

They huddled closer and stared at the door. They just didn't use another part of their bodies, and they didn't look at anything but the door. The time was past for asking the white folks what to look for through that door. Six eyes were questioning *God.*

Through the screaming wind they heard things crashing and things hurtling and dashing with unbelievable velocity. A baby rabbit, terror ridden, squirmed through a hole in the floor and squatted off there in the shadows against the wall, seeming to know that nobody wanted its flesh at such a time.

And the lake got madder and madder with only its dikes between them and him.

In a little wind-lull, Tea Cake touched Janie and said, "Ah reckon you wish now you had of stayed in yo' big house 'way from such as dis, don't yuh?"

"Naw."

"Naw?"

"Yeah, naw. People don't die till dey time come nohow, don't keer where you at. Ah'm wid mah husband in uh storm, dat's all."

"Thanky, Ma'am. But 'sposing you wuz tuh die, now. You wouldn't git mad at me for draggin' yuh heah?"

"Naw. We been tuhgether round two years. If you kin see de light at daybreak, you don't keer if you die at dusk. It's so many people never seen de light at all. Ah wuz fumblin' round and God opened de door."

He dropped to the floor and put his head in her lap. "Well then, Janie, you meant whut you didn't say, 'cause Ah never *knowed* you wuz so satisfied wid me lak dat. Ah kinda thought—"

The wind came back with triple fury, and put out the light for the last time. They sat in company with the others in other shanties, their eyes straining against crude walls and their souls asking if He meant to measure their puny might against His. They seemed to be staring at the dark, but their eyes were watching God.

As soon as Tea Cake went out pushing wind in front of him, he saw that the wind and water had given life to lots of things that folks think of as dead and given death to so much that had been living things. Water everywhere. Stray fish swimming in the yard. Three inches more and the water would be in the house. Already in some. He decided to try to find a car to take them out of the 'Glades before worse things happened. He turned back to tell Janie about it so she could be ready to go.

"Git our insurance papers tuhgether, Janie. Ah'll tote mah box mahself and things lak dat."

"You got all de money out de dresser drawer, already?"

"Naw, git it quick and cut uh piece off de table-cloth tuh wrap it up in. Us liable tuh git wet tuh our necks. Cut uh piece uh dat oilcloth quick fuh our papers. We got tuh go, if it ain't too late. De dish can't bear it out no longer."

He snatched the oilcloth off the table and took out his knife. Janie held it straight while he slashed off a strip.

"But Tea Cake, it's too awful out dere. Maybe it's better tuh stay heah in de wet than it is tuh try tuh—"

He stunned the argument with half a word. "Fix," he said and fought his way outside. He had seen more than Janie had.

Janie took a big needle and ran up a longish sack. Found some newspaper and wrapped up the paper money and papers and thrust them in and whipped over the open end with her needle. Before she could get it thoroughly hidden in the pocket of her overalls, Tea Cake burst in again.

" 'Tain't no cars, Janie."

"Ah thought not! Whut we gointuh do now?"

"We got tuh walk."

"In all dis weather, Tea Cake? Ah don't b'lieve Ah could make it out de quarters."

"Oh yeah you kin. Me and you and Motor Boat kin all lock arms and hold one 'nother down. Eh, Motor?"

"He's sleep on de bed in yonder," Janie said. Tea Cake called without moving.

"Motor Boat! You better git up from dere! Hell done broke

loose in Georgy. Dis minute! How kin you sleep at uh time lak dis? Water knee deep in de yard."

They stepped out in water almost to their buttocks and managed to turn east. Tea Cake had to throw his box away, and Janie saw how it hurt him. Dodging flying missiles, floating dangers, avoiding stepping in holes and warmed on the wind now at their backs until they gained comparatively dry land. They had to fight to keep from being pushed the wrong way and to hold together. They saw other people like themselves struggling along. A house down, here and there, frightened cattle. But above all the drive of the wind and the water. And the lake. Under its multiplied roar could be heard a mighty sound of grinding rock and timber and a wail. They looked back. Saw people trying to run in raging waters and screaming when they found they couldn't. A huge barrier of the makings of the dike to which the cabins had been added was rolling and tumbling forward. Ten feet higher and as far as they could see the muttering wall advanced before the braced-up waters like a road crusher on a cosmic scale. The monstropolous beast had left his bed. The two hundred miles an hour wind had loosed his chains. He seized hold of his dikes and ran forward until he met the quarters; uprooted them like grass and rushed on after his supposed-to-be conquerors, rolling the dikes, rolling the houses, rolling the people in the houses along with other timbers. The sea was walking the earth with a heavy heel.

"De lake is comin'!" Tea Cake gasped.

"De lake!" In amazed horror from Motor Boat, "De lake!"

"It's comin' behind us!" Janie shuddered. "Us can't fly."

"But we still kin run," Tea Cake shouted and they ran. The gushing water ran faster. The great body was held back, but rivers spouted through fissures in the rolling wall and broke like day. The three fugitives ran past another line of shanties that topped a slight rise and gained a little. They cried out as best they could, "De lake is comin'!" and barred doors flew open and others joined them in flight crying the same as they went. "De lake is comin'!" and the pursuing waters growled and shouted ahead, "Yes, Ah'm comin'!", and those who could fled on.

They made it to a tall house on a hump of ground and Janie said, "Less stop heah. Ah can't make it no further. Ah'm done give out."

"All of us is done give out," Tea Cake corrected. "We'se goin' inside out dis weather, kill or cure." He knocked with the handle of his knife, while they leaned their faces and shoulders against the wall. He knocked once more then he and Motor Boat went round to the back and forced a door. Nobody there.

"Dese people had mo' sense than Ah did," Tea Cake said as they dropped to the floor and lay there panting. "Us oughta went on wid 'Lias lak he ast me."

"You didn't know," Janie contended. "And when yuh don't know, yuh just don't know. De storms might not of come sho nuff."

They went to sleep promptly but Janie woke up first. She heard the sound of rushing water and sat up.

"Tea Cake! Motor Boat! De lake is comin'!"

The lake *was* coming on. Slower and wider, but coming. It had trampled on most of its supporting wall and lowered its front by spreading. But it came muttering and grumbling onward like a tired mammoth just the same.

"Dis is uh high tall house. Maybe it won't reach heah at all," Janie counseled. "And if it do, maybe it won't reach tuh de upstairs part."

"Janie, Lake Okechobee is forty miles wide and sixty miles long. Dat's uh whole heap uh water. If dis wind is shovin' dat whole lake disa way, dis house ain't nothin' tuh swaller. Us better go. Motor Boat!"

"Whut you want, man?"

"De lake is comin'!"

"Aw, naw it 'tain't."

"Yes it is *so* comin'! Listen! You kin hear it way off."

"It kin jus' come on. Ah'll wait right here."

"Aw, get up, Motor Boat! Less make it tuh de Palm Beach road. Dat's on uh fill. We'se pretty safe dere."

"Ah'm safe here, man. Go ahead if yuh wants to. Ah'm sleepy."

"Whut you gointuh do if de lake reach heah?"

"Go upstairs."

"S'posing it come up dere?"

"Swim, man. Dat's all."

"Well, uh, Good bye, Motor Boat. Everything is pretty bad, yuh know. Us might git missed of one 'nother. You sho is a grand friend fuh uh man tuh have."

"Good bye, Tea Cake. Y'all oughta stay here and sleep, man. No use in goin' off and leavin' me lak dis."

"We don't wanta. Come on wid us. It might be night time when de water hem you up in heah. Dat's how come Ah won't stay. Come on, man."

"Tea Cake, Ah got tuh have mah sleep. Definitely."

"Good bye, then, Motor. Ah wish you all de luck. Goin' over tuh Nassau fuh dat visit widja when all dis is over."

"Definitely, Tea Cake. Mah mama's house is yours."

Tea Cake and Janie were some distance from the house before they struck serious water. Then they had to swim a distance, and Janie could not hold up more than a few strokes at a time, so Tea Cake bore her up till finally they hit a ridge that led on towards the fill. It seemed to him the wind was weakening a little so he kept looking for a place to rest and catch his breath. His wind was gone. Janie was tired and limping, but she had not had to do that hard swimming in the turbulent waters, so Tea Cake was much worse off. But they couldn't stop. Gaining the fill was something but it was no guarantee. The lake was coming. They had to reach the six-mile bridge. It was high and safe perhaps.

Everybody was walking the fill. Hurrying, dragging, falling, crying, calling out names hopefully and hopelessly. Wind and rain beating on old folks and beating on babies. Tea Cake stumbled once or twice in his weariness and Janie held him up. So they reached the bridge at Six Mile Bend and thought to rest.

But it was crowded. White people had preempted that point of elevation and there was no more room. They could climb up one of its high sides and down the other, that was all. Miles further on, still no rest.

They passed a dead man in a sitting position on a hummock, entirely surrounded by wild animals and snakes. Common danger made common friends. Nothing sought a conquest over the other.

Another man clung to a cypress tree on a tiny island. A tin roof of a building hung from the branches by electric wires and the wind swung it back and forth like a mighty ax. The man dared not move a step to his right lest this crushing blade split him open. He dared not step left for a large rattlesnake was stretched full length with his head in the wind. There was a strip of water between the island and the fill, and the man clung to the tree and cried for help.

"De snake won't bite yuh," Tea Cake yelled to him. "He skeered tuh go intuh uh coil. Skeered he'll be blowed away. Step round dat side and swim off!"

Soon after that Tea Cake felt he couldn't walk anymore. Not right away. So he stretched long side of the road to rest. Janie spread herself between him and the wind and he closed his eyes and let the tiredness seep out of his limbs. On each side of the fill was a great expanse of water like lakes—water full of things living and dead. Things that didn't belong in water. As far as the eye could reach, water and wind playing upon it in fury. A large piece of tar-paper roofing sailed through the air and scudded along the fill until it hung against a tree. Janie saw it with joy. That was the very thing to cover Tea Cake with. She could lean against it and hold it down. The wind wasn't quite so bad as it was anyway. The very thing. Poor Tea Cake!

She crept on hands and knees to the piece of roofing and caught hold of it by either side. Immediately the wind lifted both of them and she saw herself sailing off the fill to the right, out and out over the lashing water. She screamed terribly and released the roofing which sailed away as she plunged downward into the water.

"Tea Cake!" He heard her and sprang up. Janie was trying to swim but fighting water too hard. He saw a cow swimming slowly towards the fill in an oblique line. A massive built dog was sitting on her shoulders and shivering and growling. The cow was approaching Janie. A few strokes would bring her there.

"Make it tuh de cow and grab hold of her tail! Don't use yo' feet. Jus' yo' hands is enough. Dat's right, come on!"

Janie achieved the tail of the cow and lifted her head up along the cow's rump, as far as she could above water. The cow sunk a little with the added load and thrashed a moment in terror. Thought she was being pulled down by a gator. Then she continued on. The dog stood up and growled like a lion, stiff-standing hackles, stiff muscles, teeth uncovered as he lashed up his fury for the charge. Tea Cake split the water like an otter, opening his knife as he dived. The dog raced down the back-bone of the cow to the attack and Janie screamed and slipped far back on the tail of the cow, just out of reach of the dog's angry jaws. He wanted to plunge in after her but dreaded the water, somehow. Tea Cake rose out of the water at the cow's rump and seized the dog by the neck. But he was a powerful dog and Tea Cake was over-tired. So he didn't kill the dog with one stroke as he had intended. But the dog couldn't free himself either. They fought and somehow he managed to bite Tea Cake high up on his cheek-bone once. Then Tea Cake finished him and sent him to the bottom to stay there. The cow relieved of a great weight was landing on the fill with Janie before Tea Cake stroked in and crawled weakly upon the fill again.

Janie began to fuss around his face where the dog had bitten him but he said it didn't amount to anything. "He'd uh raised hell though if he had uh grabbed me uh inch higher and bit me in mah eye. Yuh can't buy eyes in de store, yuh know." He flopped to the edge of the fill as if the storm wasn't going on at all. "Lemme rest awhile, then us got tuh make it on intuh town somehow."

It was next day by the sun and the clock when they reached Palm Beach. It was years later by their bodies. Winters and winters of hardship and suffering. The wheel kept turning round and round. Hope, hopelessness and despair. But the storm blew itself out as they approached the city of refuge.

Havoc was there with her mouth wide open. Back in the Everglades the wind had romped among lakes and trees. In the city it had raged among houses and men. Tea Cake and Janie stood on the edge of things and looked over the desolation.

"How kin Ah find uh doctor fuh yo' face in all dis mess?" Janie wailed.

"Ain't got de damn doctor tuh study 'bout. Us needs uh place tuh rest."

A great deal of their money and perseverance and they found a place to sleep. It was just that. No place to live at all. Just sleep. Tea Cake looked all around and sat heavily on the side of the bed.

"Well," he said humbly, "reckon you never 'spected tuh come tuh dis when you took up wid me, didja?"

"Once upon uh time, Ah never 'spected nothin', Tea Cake, but bein' dead from the standin' still and tryin' tuh laugh. But you come 'long and made somethin' outa me. So Ah'm thankful fuh anything we come through together."

**Zora Neale Hurston** *was born in Macon County, Alabama, in 1891. A folklorist, poet, playwright, and novelist, she published many works, including* Jonah's Gourd Vine; Moses, Man of the Mountain; Seraph on the Suwanee; *and* Their Eyes Were Watching God.

# Vacant Lot

RAYMOND E. WILLIAMS

Canyons created by small bare feet
lead to a secret world
where clover mountains are head high
when I'm lying on my back

Small harrier jets armed with stingers
hover about white ships in a green sea
while refueling themselves with nectar
they collect the yellow ore
from which their alchemists
make sweet yellow gold

The danger of attack heightens
my need to stay and watch

Below the sky-bridge of my arm
a battle wages over a crushed bee
its body the spoils of war
for the natives of my clover forest

I am in danger of mass attack
but I must stay and watch
tomorrow the mowers come

*A native of Port Arthur, Texas,* Raymond E. Williams *received a B.S. in mechanical engineering from Lamar University before becoming a computer systems analyst. He started writing only a few years ago, having been told by his high school teachers that he would never be a writer. He has had six essays published to date, and hopes to publish a novel in the near future.*

# Lost in the Swamp

## John Muir

*In the 1860s, the naturalist John Muir walked alone from Indiana to southern Florida. His account of the journey includes this description of a meeting with a southern captain living in the swamplands of western Florida. Eager to see whatever plant and animal attractions the area held, Muir gamely set out to find a special palm grove his host recommended. But the captain's suggested route, complicated and full of peril, sounds less like a pleasant side trip than like a test of Muir's survival skills!*

*October 20*

Swamp very dense during this day's journey. Almost one continuous sheet of water covered with aquatic trees and vines. No stream that I crossed to-day appeared to have the least idea where it was going. Saw an alligator plash into the sedgy brown water by the roadside from an old log.

Arrived at night at the house of Captain Simmons. . . . Our conversation, as we sat by the light of the fire, was on the one great question, slavery and its concomitants. I managed, however, to switch off to something more congenial occasionally—the birds of the neighborhood, the animals, the climate, and what spring, summer, and winter are like in these parts.

About the climate, I could not get much information, as he

had always lived in the South and, of course, saw nothing extraordinary in weather to which he had always been accustomed. But in speaking of animals, he at once became enthusiastic and told many stories of hairbreadth escapes, in the woods about his house, from bears, hungry alligators, wounded deer, etc. "And now," said he, forgetting in his kindness that I was from the hated North, "you must stay with me a few days. Deer are abundant. I will lend you a rifle and we'll go hunting. I hunt whenever I wish venison, and I can get it about as easily from the woods near by as a shepherd can get mutton out of his flock. And perhaps we will see a bear, for they are far from scarce here, and there are some big gray wolves, too."

I expressed a wish to see some large alligators. "Oh, well," said he, "I can take you where you will see plenty of those fellows, but they are not much to look at. I once got a good look at an alligator that was lying at the bottom of still, transparent water, and I think that his eyes were the most impressively cold and cruel of any animal I have seen. Many alligators go out to sea among the keys. These sea alligators are the largest and most ferocious, and sometimes attack people by trying to strike them with their tails when they are out fishing in boats.

"Another thing I wish you to see," he continued, "is a palmetto grove on a rich hummock a few miles from here. The grove is about seven miles in length by three in breadth. The ground is covered with long grass, uninterrupted with bushes or other trees. It is the finest grove of palmettos I have ever seen and I have oftentimes thought that it would make a fine subject for an artist."

I concluded to stop—more to see this wonderful palmetto hummock than to hunt. Besides, I was weary and the prospect of getting a little rest was a tempting consideration after so many restless nights and long, hard walks by day.

*October 21*

Having . . . breakfasted sumptuously on fresh venison and "caller" fish from the sea, I set out for the grand palm grove. I had seen these dazzling sun-children in every day of my walk through Florida, but they were usually standing solitary, or in groups of three or four; but to-day I was to see them by the mile. The captain led me a short distance through his corn field and showed me a trail which would conduct me to the palmy hummock. He pointed out the general direction, which I noted upon my compass.

"Now," said he, "at the other side of my farthest field you will come to a jungle of cat-briers, but will be able to pass them if you manage to keep the trail. You will find that the way is not by any means well marked, for in passing through a broad swamp, the trail makes a good many abrupt turns to avoid deep water, fallen trees, or impenetrable thickets. You will have to wade a good deal, and in passing the water-covered places you will have to watch for the point where the trail comes out on the opposite side."

I made my way through the briers, which in strength and ferocity equaled those of Tennessee, followed the path through all of its dim waverings, waded the many opposing pools, and, emerging suddenly from the leafy darkness of the swamp forest, at last stood free and unshaded on the border of the sun-drenched palm garden. It was a level area of grasses and sedges, smooth as a prairie, well starred with flowers, and bounded like a clearing by a wall of vine-laden trees.

The palms had full possession and appeared to enjoy their

sunny home. There was no jostling, no apparent effort to outgrow each other. Abundance of sunlight was there for every crown, and plenty to fall between. I walked enchanted in their midst. What a landscape! Only palms as far as the eye could reach! Smooth pillars rising from the grass, each capped with a sphere of leaves, shining in the sun as bright as a star. The silence and calm were as deep as ever I found in the dark, solemn pine woods of Canada, and that contentment which is an attribute of the best of God's plant people was as impressively felt in this alligator wilderness as in the homes of the happy, healthy people of the North. . . .

After some hours in this charming forest I started on the return journey before night, on account of the difficulties of the swamp and the brier patch. On leaving the palmettos and entering the vine-tangled, half-submerged forest I sought long and carefully, but in vain, for the trail, for I had drifted about too incautiously in search of plants. But, recollecting the direction that I had followed in the morning,

I took a compass bearing and started to penetrate the swamp in a direct line.

Of course I had a sore weary time, pushing through the tanglement of falling, standing, and half-fallen trees and bushes, to say nothing of knotted vines as remarkable for their efficient army of interlocking and lancing prickers as for their length and the number of their blossoms. But these were not my greatest obstacles, nor yet the pools and lagoons full of dead leaves and alligators. It was the army of cat-briers that I most dreaded. I knew that I would have to find the narrow slit of a lane before dark or spend the night with mosquitoes and alligators, without food or fire. The entire distance was not great, but a traveler in open woods can form no idea of the crooked and strange difficulties of pathless locomotion in these thorny, watery Southern tangles, especially in pitch darkness. I struggled hard and kept my course, leaving the general direction only when drawn aside by a plant of extraordinary promise, that I wanted for a specimen, or when I had to make the half-circuit of a pile of trees, or of a deep lagoon or pond.

In wading I never attempted to keep my clothes dry, because the water was too deep, and the necessary care would consume too much time. Had the water that I was forced to wade been transparent it would have lost much of its difficulty. But as it was, I constantly expected to plant my feet on an alligator, and therefore proceeded with strained caution. The opacity of the water caused uneasiness also on account of my inability to determine its depth. In many places I was compelled to turn back, after wading forty or fifty yards, and to try again a score of times before I succeeded in getting across a single lagoon.

At length, after miles of wading and wallowing, I arrived at the grand cat-brier encampment which guarded the whole forest in solid phalanx, unmeasured miles up and down across my way. Alas! the trail by which I had crossed in the morning was not to be found, and night was near. In vain I scrambled back and forth in search of an opening. There was not even a strip of dry ground on which to rest. Everywhere the long briers arched over to the vines and bushes of the watery swamp, leaving no standing-ground between them. I began to think of building some sort of a scaffold in a tree to rest on through the night, but concluded to make one more desperate effort to find the narrow track.

After calm, concentrated recollection of my course, I made a long exploration toward the left down the brier line, and after scrambling a mile or so, perspiring and bleeding, I discovered the blessed trail and escaped to dry land and the light. Reached the captain at sundown. Dined on milk and johnny-cake and fresh venison. Was congratulated on my singular good fortune and woodcraft, and soon after supper was sleeping the deep sleep of the weary and the safe.

*Born in Scotland,* **John Muir** *moved to the United States in 1849. He devoted most of his life to the study of natural history and to the celebration of America's wild places.*

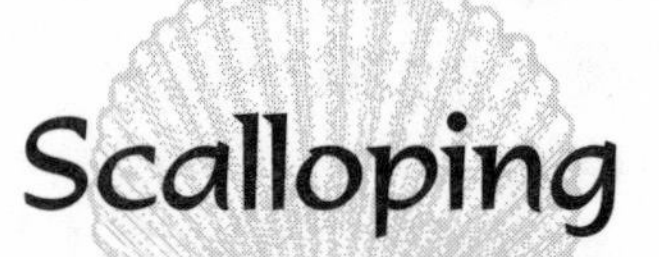

# Scalloping

ANDREANNA EDWARDS

*Sea grass beds off Florida's panhandle harbor many kinds of marine life, including abundant scallops. Most scallop hunters visit these beds in search of tasty seafood. But for others, hunting scallops is just a good excuse to go exploring.*

"I think this may be it," my brother says, pointing to the clear water off to our left. My father cuts the motor and we drift. The morning air is salty and wet around us.

"You really think this is The Spot?" he asks.

"Maybe." My brother nods his head.

"You're right," I agree, staring past the water's glassy ripples. Patches of green sea grass soften the sandy bottom. "The grass isn't too thick," I say, watching the long, thin blades bend to expose the ocean floor.

"And it looks just deep enough." My mother sits next to me and leans over the boat's side. We are all looking for signs that this could indeed be The Spot.

After a few minutes of waiting and watching, I notice a pale, round shell resting on top of the dark sea grass.

"There's one!" I yell.

"There's another!" my brother shouts. "And another!"

Suddenly, everyone is busy grabbing masks, snorkels, and

net bags, rubbing suntan lotion over exposed shoulders and backs, and lacing up old tennis shoes. We've found The Spot. It's time to scallop.

Scalloping is a traditional summertime activity for my family. Each July and August we make several trips to St. Joseph's Bay, located off the Florida panhandle. We spend the day snorkeling and gathering scallops to clean and cook later for a special family meal. No matter how many or how few scallops we find, each trip is filled with adventure and discovery and enough entertaining stories to last through the summer.

After raising the red safety flag, which alerts boaters to nearby swimmers, I jump into the waist-high water with a splash. My shoes sink into the spongy bottom. Already, I feel a lump under my right foot. Reaching down, I untangle the slick blades of grass and carefully lift what I hope will be the first scallop of the day. No such luck. I stare at the prickly sea urchin sitting on my palm and remember why wearing tennis shoes is such a good idea.

As my father anchors the boat, I tug on my mask and snorkel and stretch out, floating on my stomach. Lying like this, I feel suspended between two very different worlds. Above me, the hot July sun warms my back and I hear the steady sounds of gulls and boat motors. Below me, the water is cool, and the grass sways silently in the current.

I spy another scallop snuggled in the grass and decide to completely enter the underwater world. Kicking my feet and holding my breath, I dive below to retrieve it. Water fills my ears and my hair fans out around me. This must be what it's like to be a mermaid, I

think. I grab the scallop and continue swimming along the ocean's bottom, parting the grass as I go. Whoa! I'm surprised by a face-to-face meeting with an ugly mud fish! He darts away into a cloud of mud and silt. I let myself drift up to the surface and blow water out of my snorkel. And this must be what it's like to be a dolphin.

I float along the surface for a while, scanning the bottom and listening to the rhythm of my breath rushing in and out of the snorkel. The water deepens as I pass over one of the many holes that pock the bay. Passing over a sandbar, I notice several hermit crabs and the faint outline of a stingray buried in the white sand.

I float back over the grass again. Dozens of fish dart between the blades. Soon I happen upon a pair of armored horseshoe crabs. I dive below to take a closer look at these prehistoric creatures and imagine they are looking back at me with each of their four eyes. Horseshoe crabs have two small eyes up front and two large ones on the sides of their shells. A long, pointed tail extends from the back of each crab. Though it looks intimidating, I know the tail is harmless and mainly used by the crab to turn itself over when it gets flipped on its back. I tap one crab's smooth, hard shell as if to say good-bye, and swim up to the surface.

Whoosh! I blow the water out of my snorkel and it falls around my head and shoulders like rain. It takes a moment to catch my breath. Out of the corner of my eye, I notice movement. It's a scallop swimming. Over and over, the mollusk clamps its two fanlike shells together, squirting water out of one side and moving in the other direction. The scallop pauses for a moment and, without the force from its clamping shells, begins to sink. Now's the time to grab it, I think—no risk of getting a finger pinched. But I don't. Instead, I remain still, watching. And just seconds before it reaches the ocean's bottom, the scallop resumes clamping its shells and jets forward again.

I won't take this scallop. No, not this one. I'll just follow along behind it, with my half-empty net bag, waiting to be led to my next discovery.

*As a child,* **Andreanna Edwards** *never lived more than a hop, skip, and jump from the ocean. Scalloping, chasing ghost crabs at dusk, and treasure hunting along the sand dunes were some of her favorite pastimes. Those discoveries and adventures are now the inspiration for many of the stories and articles Mrs. Edwards loves to write.*

# Southern Winter

CHRISTA PANDEY

We love those flakes that visit us
In odd years and blue moons,
When school is closed for icy ways
And we prepare for make-up days
While watching old cartoons.

Sometimes the stuff falls long enough
To build a snowman here,
But when we roll the balls up tight
For creatures barely half our height
We scrape the green lawn clear.

**Christa Pandey** *has lived in two Gulf Coast states for a total of twenty-five years. In all of that time she has never had enough snow to build the majestic snowmen she remembers from her childhood.*

# Searching for Ed Palmer

ROB KERR

*Have you ever thought about what your community was like before you came along? It is sometimes easy to forget that the buildings and people you know now weren't always there, that a long history precedes your own residency in a place. But if you take a closer look at the names of places in your community, you may uncover clues to the people and events of long ago.*

People say it's hard to believe a thirteen-year-old girl would sail out into Galveston Bay all alone at night searching for the place where a man she never knew drowned, but that's what I did and it's the truth.

My name is Sophie Palmer Davenport, and it all started when I asked my father where my middle name came from. I was curious if there might be some connection between my name and a fishing spot near our bay house called Palmer's Pier. It's just a dilapidated old set of pilings, but I've always teased my brother, Nathan, by saying the pier belongs to me and he better ask my permission whenever he wants to fish over there.

Place names interest me. I always wonder how and why a certain place got its name, and what the story is behind it. Take Buffalo Bayou, for instance, which runs right through the middle of Houston and empties into Galveston Bay. I suppose herds of wild buffalo must have roamed its banks at one time. Sometimes when I'm out in my sailboat, I gaze along the shore of the bay and try to imagine Indians on their ponies chasing the hairy beasts as they would have done before the highways, office buildings, and subdivisions came along.

My dad didn't know anything about the history of Palmer's Pier. He said it had always been called that and looked the same now as when he was a boy. My name, he said, came down through his family somehow. If anything, he thought there could be a connection between my name and Palmer Episcopal Church on Main Street in Houston, which my family has attended for as long as I can remember. He told me that Palmer Church is unusual because it's about the only Episcopal Church in the United States named after a regular person rather than somebody or something out of the Bible. It's named after a man who drowned in Galveston Bay in 1908, whose sister built the church in his honor. Palmer Church is an Italian-style church located between Hermann Park and Rice University. My mom says it's about the prettiest church and location in Houston.

The man who drowned was Edward Palmer. My dad told me that he thought one of our ancestors probably knew him, because the name Palmer first appears in our family tree around 1910, soon after Ed Palmer died. It gave me goose bumps when he told me that and made me wonder if I might have some sort of spiritual connection to Ed Palmer. Sometimes I can get really interested in things that are spooky or eerie, and right off I wanted to find out more about Ed Palmer and his drowning.

A few weeks later I asked Nathan to take me to the

downtown library on Saturday afternoon to do research about the drowning. I wouldn't normally go to the library unless I needed to for school, but this was a special case. Nathan doesn't believe in psychic things and he thought I was nutty. But he didn't mind taking me because he just turned sixteen and got his driver's license and is happy for any excuse to borrow Mom's car.

Nathan rolled his blue eyes and said, "All right, let's go."

"This will be interesting," I said optimistically.

"I bet," he said with a laugh as we walked out the door.

I had learned how to research old newspaper articles for a school project last year, and I was excited to have a chance to do it again for something I thought up all by myself. When we got to the library, Nathan and I looked up the *Houston Post* newspapers on microfiche for the year 1908 until we found a bunch of articles about the drowning.

We learned that Ed Palmer was twenty-five when he drowned, on August 7, 1908. According to the newspaper article that came out a couple days later, *he was a man of flawless honor and integrity and of marked devotion to duty . . . and at his death was the assistant cashier of the First National Bank of Houston.* It's funny how the newspapers were so personal and their language so flowery in those days. It makes the people sound more interesting and romantic than the people you read about in the paper now.

Reading one of the articles through the viewfinder, I was amazed to see that Ed Palmer drowned in Seabrook, because that's near where my family's bay house is. And to top it off, the article said my great-grandfather was present when it happened. I felt a chill go down my spine when I read that. My father was right—we did have a family connection to Ed Palmer!

Nathan said it was just another coincidence and no big deal, but I was becoming fascinated with the story and printed out the articles to take with me to the bay the following weekend.

Galveston Bay was a favorite place for Houstonians to go for recreation back in the early 1900s. It still is, but a lot of my friends and their families go to Galveston Island instead because it has a beach. The bay is closer to Houston, though, and back in the old days it was a lot easier to get to. Our house is made out of wood and must be a hundred years old. It's right on the water and has a little dock where we can keep our boats and catch fish and crabs in crab traps. I have a sailboat called an Optimist, but I'm almost too big for it now and for Christmas I hope to get a Sunfish like Nathan has.

Seabrook—where Ed Palmer drowned—lies on the edge of Galveston Bay where it meets a large lake called Clear Lake. Clear Lake is best known as the home of NASA. All the astronauts live around there. A big bridge spans the channel connecting Clear Lake to the bay, and there are five or six restaurants lined up along the channel where people can eat seafood and watch the shrimp boats, sailboats, and motor boats go by. Clear Lake has never seemed very clear to me, so I can't figure out why it's called that unless it's in comparison to the bay itself, which is usually pretty muddy and murky.

Long before there were astronauts and before there was a big bridge over the channel, people had little houses and docks on Clear Lake and on the bay, and some—like my family—still do. We usually spend the whole summer at the bay. I like to race my Optimist in local regattas, and I've won more than a few. We love to fish for speckled trout right off our dock, and set out crab traps. These square traps are made out of chicken wire. We put raw chicken necks in them and toss the traps off the dock for a few hours. The crabs find their way into the traps through an opening, but they aren't smart enough to get out.

When we arrived at our bay house late on Friday afternoon, Nathan and I went down to the dock and set our crab traps. After dinner, we turned on our dock lights, which shine on the water and attract speckled trout. Nathan caught two specks and I caught three that night, using live bait shrimp we bought at Pete's Bait and Supply in Seabrook on the way down from Houston. It was relaxing just sitting on the dock with my line in the water, watching the stars and listening to the water lap up against the pilings of the dock. I found myself thinking about Ed Palmer. He would have seen the same stars and heard the same sounds. Maybe he set out crab traps and fished from a dock, too.

Nathan and I were pleased with our catch and with the dozen or so crabs we snared in our trap. As we cleaned the fish, we decided to cook the entire dinner for our parents and their friends who were coming to visit the next night. We spent much of Saturday afternoon preparing the meal. We broiled the fish in lemon and butter and boiled the crabs in a big pot with corn-on-the-cob and new potatoes. We served our dinner with French bread, on newspapers spread out on the long pine table on our screened-in porch, along with bottles of ice-cold root beer. The sun was going down over the bay, the Gulf breeze was blowing, and my parents' friends said they had no idea there was a place this close to Houston that was so enjoyable in the summertime.

At bedtime, Nathan and I decided to sleep in the two hammocks on the screened-in porch, where the ceiling fan keeps the air moving. The Saint Augustine grass in front of the porch slopes down to the water. I got out the articles from the *Houston Post* and turned on the lamp we keep on the porch for reading. The air from the fan played with my hair.

"Nathan," I said, "listen to this—*Mr. Palmer was of a party of pleasure-seekers who had been enjoying the regatta during the day aboard the* Gypsy Girl. *Last night at approximately eleven o'clock they were returning to Seabrook after a pleasure sail. When near Bailey's Pier at Seabrook, Miss Daphne Palmer fell overboard."*

"Too bad," Nathan mumbled, half asleep.

"Have you ever heard of Bailey's Pier, Nathan?"

The only sound was Nathan sawing logs. I jumped up and shook him. "Where is Bailey's Pier?"

"Never heard of it, Sofe." Nathan returned to sawing logs.

I was annoyed. Nathan and I knew the names of most everything in the Seabrook area, but we had never heard of the place where Ed Palmer—my soul mate, you might say—drowned. I read on, itching to learn more about the tragic accident. The article said several men jumped in the water to try to rescue Miss Daphne Palmer. One of them was my great-grandfather, Farrell Davenport, and another was Miss Palmer's brother, Ed. *Miss Palmer was taken aboard the* Gypsy Girl, *where restoratives were administered, but Ed Palmer has not been seen since he leaped into the water. The joy of the safe rescue of Miss Daphne Palmer was soon forgotten in the sorrow that fell upon all at Seabrook when a hasty roll call showed Ed Palmer to be missing. Every possible search was made for him, but he was not located and at once dragging commenced, which continued all night in the hope of finding the body.*

Several articles I read gave details about Ed Palmer's life. Reading them made me teary. He sounded like a hard-working, honest man.

On Monday, I decided to pay a small tribute to the memory

of Ed Palmer by naming my own boat the *Gypsy Girl.* I rode my bike down to Pete's Bait and Supply to buy stenciled boat letters for my Optimist. Pete's was just a shack on the edge of Seabrook, but it always seemed to have whatever you needed for any bay activity. Old Pete himself, thin as a wire and puffing on his pipe, was making a pyramid out of bait buckets on the porch when I pedaled up.

"If it ain't Miss Sophie Davenport," he drawled. "What can I do for you?"

I told him what I needed and he led me to the aisle where stencils were kept. Then it occurred to me that Old Pete had seen it all. Maybe he would know. "Pete, have you ever heard of Bailey's Pier?"

Pete stuffed his hands in his pockets and furrowed his brow. "I sure have, though I can't recall the last time anyone called it by that name."

"Well, where is it?" I asked excitedly.

"What's left of it is just across the water, near Johnny's Crab Shack."

"You mean near Palmer's Pier?" I asked.

"Well, sort of." He took two quick puffs. "You see, Bailey's Pier and Palmer's Pier are one and the same. The tale I heard is that after the Palmer boy drowned years back, folks began to call it Palmer's Pier, kinda in honor like."

I was astounded. I knew exactly where Ed Palmer drowned, and it was right by the pier I liked to think belonged to me!

The next night, I again slept in the hammock. Nathan and my mom were sleeping inside where the window air conditioner kept you cool. Dad had gone back to Houston for the workweek. I drifted in and out of sleep. The moon wasn't full, but it was bright, and the sky was cloudless. As I gazed at the moonlight dancing on the gentle waves of the bay, I realized that the date was August 7, 2001, exactly ninety-three years since Ed Palmer drowned.

I turned on the lamp and read a bit more from one of the articles. *There is an added pathos about his death in the fact that, upon his father's death, young Palmer was left the only representative of his name.* I looked up *pathos* in the dictionary and learned it means something that causes pity or sadness. Ed Palmer's story certainly did that to me. And I realized that *I* was probably now the only representative of his name. I felt an irresistible urge to go to the place where he drowned and say a prayer for him. If I hurried, I thought, I could sail my Optimist over to Palmer's Pier by eleven o'clock, the hour Ed Palmer had drowned.

I'd sailed at night before, but of course I wasn't allowed to go out alone. This time, though, no one was going to stop me. I tiptoed out the screen door, picked a yellow rose from the bush in front of the porch, and grabbed my red life jacket from the boathouse. I sneaked down to the dock. It may have been wrong and dangerous, but I did it anyway.

As I was rigging up the *Gypsy Girl,* putting in the mast and attaching the rudder, I noticed clouds gathering. My sail was whipping around as I adjusted the sprit pole and lowered the boat into the shallow water. The wind was steadily increasing. Good, I thought, I can reach Palmer's Pier faster. But I had no idea a late summer thunderstorm was rapidly approaching.

I'd sailed half a mile or so downwind toward Palmer's Pier before I realized the moonlight was gone. The temperature dropped suddenly and the waves grew. Droplets of water sprinkled down from the pitch-black sky. The wind strengthened and salt water slapped against the bow of the *Gypsy Girl.* My stomach tightened with fear. I was almost to Palmer's Pier when a bolt of lightning flashed very near me. Then another, the thunder crashing only a split second after the lightning struck.

I'd planned to commune with Ed Palmer's spirit, so to speak, to let him know he was still remembered, that we had a spiritual connection and shared a name and a special place. But now I felt only fear for my own situation. I tossed the yellow rose into the water, mumbled something like "May you rest in peace," and jibed to head for home.

My timing couldn't have been worse. Just as I pushed the tiller a gust of wind whipped my sail around and the *Gypsy Girl* tipped over. I fell into the churning bay. The clouds blocked the moonlight so that I could barely see, but I quickly realized my boat had "turtled." The mast was pointing straight down and was stuck in the muddy bottom. It's hard enough to right a turtled Optimist in the easiest of conditions, but on a stormy, dark night like this I knew I couldn't do it. Even if I could, I wouldn't be able to sail the *Gypsy Girl* with the sheets of rain that were beating down. I floated in the water holding on to the overturned hull, depending on my life jacket to keep me afloat. Lightning continued to strike. I was terrified to be in the water in such a violent thunderstorm, but all I could do was wait it out and pray that nothing awful would happen.

A few moments later, I heard my name called out. Through the pounding rain and choppy waves I saw Nathan's Sunfish. He must have seen me leave our dock and had come after me. I'd never been so relieved! At the same time I felt ashamed for getting caught doing something so dumb. Nathan slowly but skillfully maneuvered his Sunfish toward me through the rain and gusts of wind. His hair lay flat against his wet forehead. When he was within arm's reach, I noticed that he didn't have his life jacket on. He never went out without it—especially at night. I guessed that in his hurry to catch up with me he hadn't had time to get it from the boathouse.

"Here—climb aboard!" he shouted. "We'll worry about the Optimist later!"

I let go of the *Gypsy Girl* and reached for his outstretched hand.

"Sophie, what in the world were you doing?"

"I'm sorry, Nathan" was all I could say.

He tugged on my hand, but somehow lost his balance and slipped off the Sunfish. As he slid into the water, his head knocked against the *Gypsy Girl.* And the Sunfish, freed suddenly from Nathan's weight, tipped over in the opposite direction. I looked back for Nathan, but a wave splashed my face, stinging my eyes. Squinting, I saw his head bob a few feet away and then—to my horror—sink underwater.

"Nathan!"

I dived as far underwater as my life jacket would allow me to go and groped wildly in all directions for him. I opened my eyes wide, but could see only blackness.

After what felt like an eternity, my foot bumped his shoulder. I reached down, grabbed hold, and pulled with all my might. I finally raised his head above water and, working my arms under his armpits from behind, leaned back and floated so that we could both breathe. Nathan is tall, but luckily he's skinny. In a few moments he came to.

As fast as it had started, the rain stopped and the wind died down. Together, Nathan and I righted our sailboats and sailed in silence back to our bay house.

The next morning, Nathan woke me in the hammock. I had slept late and the sun was blinding. "I was going to tell Mom what you did last night," he said, "but I changed my mind."

"Why?"

"There's really no point, Sofe. I think you've learned your lesson the hard way."

Nathan was right. Sure, it was exciting to get close to Ed Palmer's spirit, but I hoped I'd never again get *that* close.

I'm still fascinated by the story of Ed Palmer, even more so now that I almost doomed my brother to Ed's same fate in the same place on the same day of the year. Sometimes when I sail past Palmer's Pier I can almost hear the laughter of Ed, Daphne, my great-grandfather, and their friends aboard the *Gypsy Girl.* I want to warn them, to somehow reach across the years and the water and prevent the accident. And though I know I can't, I believe that somehow Ed knows I am here and thinking of him as I live my life in the same places he once knew well. Maybe Ed Palmer and all those who came before us and whose hopes and fears and dreams live on in the names of towns and rivers and mountains know we follow behind them, tying our lives and stories into the landscape along with their own.

**Rob Kerr** *has published six short stories in the last year and recently completed two young adult novels. He lives in Houston with his wife and four daughters, several of whom enjoy sailing in Galveston Bay.*

Great Places

# Crazy

ANGELA JOHNSON

You'd have to be
crazy
to want to live
your life in
a place like Shorter, Alabama.
The heat,
the red ants, and
twenty miles to
any mall.
You'd have to be crazy
to want to live
in a place where
every other person is
related to you
and thinks they know
everything about your
life.
You'd have to be crazy
to want to wake
up every morning to sweet
magnolia and moist red

dirt.
You'd have to be
crazy.

*A native of Alabama,* **Angela Johnson** *is the author of many picture books and novels, including* Toning the Sweep, *a Coretta Scott King Award Book, and* When I Am Old with You, *a Coretta Scott King Honor Book. She currently lives in Kent, Ohio.*

# The Singing River

## Sylvia B. Williams

*Many of the stories we tell to make sense of the natural world come to us from science. But others come from indigenous communities that have wrestled with the very same mysteries, such as why the Pascagoula River hums and sings.*

The Pascagoula River, sometimes called the Singing River, flows through the town of Pascagoula, Mississippi, and empties into the Gulf of Mexico. The town and the river got their name from the Pascagoula Indian tribe who lived there many years ago.

People who live near the Pascagoula say it makes a humming sound deep in the water. Others say it sounds like someone singing. Why would a river sound like it's making music?

From time to time, people have tried to find the location of the sound by riding in a boat all the way to the mouth of the river. The music is said to be loudest at sundown. It is also said to be loudest in the hot summer months.

People who hear the music have a hard time describing how it sounds. One time the sound seems to come from under their boat. Another time it seems like a giant bumblebee buzzing around their ears. Sometimes it seems to come from the left bank of the river, then from the right bank.

Many people, including scientists, have tried to explain this mysterious music. One explanation is that it's a trick of underwater currents and marsh gas moving along the sand. Another is that it's the sound made by a species of fish swimming in the river. Scientists have also thought it might be sand grating on a hard slate bottom, or water flowing through a hidden cave.

So far, no one has been able to prove any of these scientific explanations. An old Indian legend explains the Singing River like this:

Long ago the Pascagoula Indians lived near the Gulf of Mexico beside the Pascagoula River. They hated a neighboring tribe, the Biloxi, who were always on the warpath.

One day Olustee, son of the Pascagoula chief, went on a hunting trip. While in the woods, he saw Miona, daughter of the Biloxi chief, as she and her friends were picking berries. He could not take his eyes off her beautiful face and velvet brown eyes. She stared at Olustee, a strong, handsome brave. They began to meet by the river and soon fell in love.

Olustee asked Miona to come with him. "My people will love you just as I love you," he told her. With tears in her eyes, she told him that her father had pledged her to Otanga, a fierce warrior of the Biloxi tribe. She was afraid to tell her father that she loved a brave from the Pascagoula tribe.

Olustee pleaded with Miona to be his bride. Finally, her love for him proved stronger than her fear of her father. She ran away with him to his tribe.

Olustee's father, the great chief, was charmed by Miona's beauty and gentleness. He and the Pascagoula tribe thought she would be a fit bride for their future chief. Olustee's father planned a big wedding celebration to take place the next day.

When Otanga heard that his bride-to-be had run away with

Olustee, he was furious. He went to her father, and they decided to attack the Pascagoula tribe. They sneaked into the Pascagoula camp at night and attacked while everyone was sleeping.

The Biloxi warriors outnumbered the Pascagoula warriors. Though the Pascagoula warriors fought hard, Olustee saw that his tribe would be conquered. He told them, "Hand me over to the Biloxi since I am the cause of the fighting."

But Miona said, "Otanga wants only me. Give me to him, and he will leave you alone."

The brave Pascagoula warriors swore to save Olustee and his bride or perish with them. They vowed that they would never let their worst enemy, the Biloxi, conquer them.

Olustee told his father, "It is better for us to live in the deep water than be killed by the Biloxi or made into their slaves."

"That is true, Olustee," said his father. The Pascagoula chief then cried out, "Men, women, and children of the Pascagoula, let us walk into the river where the Biloxi can attack us no longer."

So, when all hope was gone, the women and children led the way into the river, the braves following. Then came Olustee and his beautiful Miona. All joined hands and marched into the waters of the Pascagoula River, singing and chanting—chanting their death song. The waves rose and fell, gently joining the death song of the Pascagoula Indian tribe as they walked deeper and deeper into the river.

Anyone who listened closely could also hear a song coming from the ocean waters of the Gulf of Mexico. This song, too, joined the song of the Pascagoulas. But it was not a song of death. It was a song of life, of another land where there was no war or hatred.

To this day, the echoes of the Pascagoula tribe's death song are said to be heard along the banks of the river, the Pascagoula, the Singing River.

It has also been said, however, that if the Pascagoula tribe did walk into the river, they must have come out on the other side. For it has been documented that there were Pascagoula Indians still living in the area in the early part of the nineteenth century. Now that sounds like another story!

**Sylvia B. Williams** *is the author of three biographies for children:* Leontyne Price: Opera Superstar *(Childrens Press, 1984),* Alex Haley: I Have A Dream *(Abdo and Daughters, 1996), and* Paul "Bear" Bryant: Football Legend *(Seacoast Publishing, 2001). She lives in West Point, Mississippi.*

# Into the Bayous

NORBERT KRAPF

*For Sonja and in memory of Sid Dupois*

Storm-brown bayou waters
gurgling in the motor's throat
swell beneath the boat.
On both sides of the bayou
dark green cypress trees
shimmering with silvery moss
wobble on knees creeping
toward the bottom of the channel.
Between bobbing lavender water
hyacinths a snowy egret lifts
spindly legs out of muddy water,
flaps wings in slow motion,
and blurs into a blue sky.
We cut the motor and glide
in cool shadows beneath
pig pecans and live oaks
twined with muscadine vines
toward the small island where
squirrels bark and wild
goats stray. Landed, we feed

and bathe on a blanket of leaves
in the few drops of sunlight
that penetrate the dark
foliage. I drift off to sleep
and dream I'm a whiskered catfish
skimming my belly across the mud
at the bottom of the bayous.

**Norbert Krapf** *is the author of several collections of poetry, including* Blue-Eyed Grass: Poems of Germany, Somewhere in Southern Indiana, *and* Bittersweet Along the Expressway. *His wife is a Cajun from Lafayette, Louisiana.*

# The Lure of the Swamp

JOHN CUTRONE

*The Florida Everglades is the largest flooded grassland in the world. Its water holes attract fish, frogs, and crocodiles. Its marshes attract crowds of wading birds. And all this attracts people curious about the wilder corners of our world.*

When I was in the ninth grade, I wrote a term paper on the Florida Everglades. It was my first real research paper. I learned to use the *Reader's Guide to Periodical Literature* and came up with an article on the Glades from a *National Geographic* published in the late 1950s. It was an expansive article, expansive like the watery land it spoke of, full of swampy photographs dripping with the greens, blues, and yellows of another time.

For weeks I kept returning to the library just to look at that article. It was the lurking wildness that I loved about my home state, all that swampiness waiting beneath the concrete. It sparked my curiosity. And when I asked my folks to take me to the Glades, they took me to the boardwalks of Corkscrew Swamp.

For a coastal boy accustomed only to sand and pelicans, it was an adventure into the unknown. I saw things up close that I'd only seen in books: cypress knees, swamp lilies, the amazing abundance of bromeliads perched high in the trees, thriving off air and water. Here was the saw grass I had read about, and the awkward anhinga drying its wings in the sun, just like in the photographs. The anhinga is a fishing bird that, oddly enough, cannot fly with wet wings. It sits there patiently at the water's edge, black wings outstretched, a bit like a phoenix but somehow not nearly as majestic. Herons and egrets with pointed bills walked on stilts across lettuce lakes—fresh water covered entirely by crimped green leaves. They stepped so gingerly across them as to never force a ripple, while eyes watched from beneath the surface—round eyes that barely blinked and you couldn't be sure if they were attached to fish or frog or gator or who knows what.

And there *were* gators: three or four of the mean, ferocious variety that pass the hours lazily warming themselves atop a sunny log or a floating bank of peat. And in the stillness of the place, there was the grand railroad-station chatter of the roosting wood storks that began as a mere buzzing early on and grew steadily louder till we thought we might be running headlong into a swarm of bees. But no, it was wood storks, more than we could count, big clumsy birds perched high in the trees, talking madly to each other and doing what roosting wood storks do.

But mostly, there was something about the cypress, something I couldn't quite grasp. Something about the quality of sunlight as it filtered through those ancient trees. Like coming in from outside, into a room of gray-headed grandfathers, most of them tall, some of them soaking their feet, knees propped up, each one silent yet brimming with tales of days gone by, tales only they know, tales in their own native tongue, tales leaning close to vanishing.

Since those days when I was a boy, my family has moved its homestead to a place some fifteen miles in from the Atlantic coast. Here, the wading birds are a more common sight than the pelicans, the soil is muckier, and quite often alligators bellow from the pond at night. But still, Corkscrew beckons from across the peninsula. When I go, I know exactly where I am, and despite the lure of the lettuce lakes, my favorite part is the pond cypress swamp. The place is thick with those same *National Geographic* colors, circa 1958. The trees exhale cool air. Sometimes, if no one is around, I just lay myself down on that boardwalk and breathe it all in, all those greens and blues and yellows. And no matter how much of it I take in, it still leaves me breathless.

**John Cutrone** *is a letterpress printer and bookbinder. He gardens and writes when he can at his home beneath a mango tree near Florida's Lake Worth Lagoon.*

# Still Weather

## Carol Munn

You, too, would be sedated by damp air, muggy grass,
rising cicada whir, bobwhites always answering each
other's call like children in the corner pool emerging
blind calling *Marco!* answered by *Polo!* to find out
where they are. I am finally home.

**Carol Munn** *won an Academy of American Poets Prize and two fellowship competitions while earning her M.F.A. in creative writing at the University of Michigan in Ann Arbor. After teaching in Spain for two years, she returned to her native Texas to teach English in northwest Houston.*

# Where the Wild Animals Is Plentiful

MAY JORDAN

*May Jordan lived for most of her life with her parents and seven siblings on a farm in southwestern Alabama. Her father earned extra income as a fur trader, and May sometimes helped him collect furs from local hunters. In the following excerpts, taken from journals written in 1912 and 1913, May describes those trips and shares her keen, sometimes wry, impressions of her Alabama homeland.*

I am A little Alabama Girl living on the Frontier Where the Wild animals is plentiful. My home is on Log Run the waters of Pine Barren I have a beautiful home. The shade trees is Cedar and China trees. In the summer when the roses are in bloom It is the Prettiest Place on the old State Line road. We have Cape Jessamines And orange blossoms for Bouquets I think the fig trees is beautiful. The Pear trees are in bloom now. There is no change in the color of the Pines they are always green. Our church is two miles Away. It is A Baptist church. . . . Well Boys I am going to give you my experiences on buying furs through Alabama And my Adventures with animals And the history of the country as seen by an Alabama girl. I have lived in sunny Dixie Land for 8 years and sure love the Land of flowers. My Dear Father and Mother was borned and raised and married in Braken County Kentucky and then moved to Adams County Ohio And there I was Borned[.] Part of my sisters and brothers was borned in central Ohio and Part in Kentucky and two here in the bright and sunny South where the Mocking birds sings all the time And where the sleigh bells never Jingle

Now I will tell you of the first trip after furs commencing DEC 1. SUNDAY I spent at home And A Jolly time.

And then MONDAY [DECEMBER] 2 at home It rained so we could not go.

TUESDAY [DECEMBER] 3 we started for the Koenton settlement Traveling the St Stephens and State Line road one mile west of home then we turned to the right and come to the Chatom and Koenton road we Journeyed onward to Mr Joe Phillips [Philips] and got A coon hide from him . . . And then on to Mr. Bud Carpenters and got furs to A finish and then we come to camp close to Mr Carpenters. And while I was cooking supper Papa went to Mr Willie Irbys and got furs to A finish. And he sure looked funny coming back with the coon hides swinging on his back. Well the country is broken. The timber is principaly pine. We had company Mr. Carpenters folks and certainly enjoyed their company. Well after they went home we had A very close shave with A wildcat but managed to get him in the wagon with us.

Well FRIDAY [DECEMBER] 6 we started for Chatom and turned to the left and went by the old Chatom schoolhouse and went to Mrs Maggie Mosses and got furs and then we come back to the schoolhouse and camped there. It is A very pretty place with its pretty grove of shade trees But very lonely. We passed A very pleasant night And got furs from her boys. Coons fox and skunk. Mrs Mosses folks are very clever people. Well I sure enjoyed my first trip But then I enjoyed my self better after I got better Acquainted.

WED DEC. 11 On our road to Mcintosh [McIntosh] Through A Very lonely country We never seen Any one For A day and A half. All we seen was A Panthers and Bears and deers.

[MONDAY] DEC 30 At Mr. Noah Howards home He had the following furs. Bear Lynx Panther Badger Otter Beaver skunk Wildcat civet Pine Marten Foxes Opossum Raccoon Mink Weasel.

[FRIDAY] JAN 3 At home[.] We was cought in A cyclone Last night.

[WEDNESDAY] JAN. 15. On Toiler [Tauler] Creek 5 miles of home Land Broken. The alligators is thick We Landed one 5 ft Long.

[THURSDAY] JAN. 16. 5 mi south of Chatom close to Fairhope Church on our way to Tibbie[.] it is raining today I am cooking in the rain[.] I am setting on A cross tie Papa is setting in the wagon.

Well TUESDAY MORNING [JANUARY 28] and on the way to Bigbee[.] Well the road is in very good condistion so far no boggy places. . . . We have not seen Any game to speak of only A Jaybird And redbird and cows and sheep And A hog. He had to walk on crutches He was so fat. . . .

Well. FRIDAY MORNING JAN 31. On our way to Mr. Noah Howards Over A very reasonable road. We journeyed Part of our way through the belt of Timber known as the Widow Sages Timber it [is?] A very beautiful sight the Pines is Always bright and green And when the sun is shining the needles just Glistens. We cooked dinner beside the road[.] . . .

SUNDAY MORNING [FEBRUARY 2 1913] We are on our way to Chatom And home. We had to camp for it is raining And We are cold I am shivering so I cant hardly write[.] We are 2 miles south of Chatom close to Mr. Baxters. The wind is blowing cold. We are on A ridge where the wind will shave A man[.] Papa never shaved when he got home. Well Mama I will have to go to the fire or I will freeze Bye, Bye to All.

TUESDAY [FEBRUARY] 11. Well good morning to All. This is A very pleasant morning We are in A beautiful grove of pines and sweetgums Close to Mr. Milton McDowells home. . . . Papa and I are setting Around the campfire of rosen pine. It is just breaking day[.] We crossed Sentibo [Santa Bogue] it is certainly A beautiful creek And A beautiful surroundings The Spanish Moss is hanging on the Trees. And the Beautiful Magnolias trees is certainly A beautiful sight And the Live oaks is certainly odd they tell when there is rain or a storm coming. They are delicate green on the upper side of the Leaf and white on the under side. And when there is A storm coming they turn the white side upwards. And It is A sign that never fails. . . . The country we have traveled to get here is so rough and Hilly that the Rabbits has to Lean Against the trees to make Ashadow. Also they are trying to in vent some way to get

from one Hill to the other without trying to walk. And the Mosquitoes is so bad they will carry A stranger Away. . . .

Well good morning to All. This is THURSDAY [FEBRUARY] 13. And cloudy and cold[.] We Went to Mr. B. A. Millers this morning and bought furs. Skunk opossum and Raccoon. And sure had A pleasant time They are very clever People. He has A pretty Daughter. Every body is busy chopping lighter to make fires. I am Alone now Papa has gone to Mr. Jacksons two miles And A half[.] The country is cleared here Everybody is farming[.] The timber is oak and pine. Well sir Just Listen And I will tell you something We got in the Hills And the rabbits started to run down the Hills And they went so fast that they bounced And turned somer saults And Knocked their Brains out Against the rocks and stumps And all we had to do was to Pick them up when we got to the bottom. Now just think of that[.] . . .

FRIDAY [FEBRUARY] 14. Good morning And how is All this morning. This is the coldest morning we have had this winter[.] Ice freezes in the Pans and buckets as soon As the fire is shut away from them[.] I am sitting by the fire by myself Papa is Asleep now. We Passed the Mount Caremal [Carmel] Church And it was A Pretty sight The Spanish Moss certainly was beautiful swinging in the wind. You have often heard of the moss hanging on the rock but here it hangs on the trees. Well day is breaking And the Dawn is Pretty All colors that no artist can Paint. The sun never seems to rise twice in the direction scince we have been camping. This is A good farming country here around Healing Springs. The chickens is crowing for day and the country is sure ringing. There is plenty of Wild animals here such as Wildcats Bear Wolves and Panther And Dear and wildturkey and other small Animals. We are on the frontier of Alabama Where we have some wild People And then we have good People here You know it takes all kinds of people to Make the world. . . .

Well good morning This is TUESDAY [FEBRUARY] 18 And smooth cloudy. We are both very well[.] We had Bad Luck last night our mule Broke loose and is gone Papa is hunting her this morning. I am Alone 3 miles from Bigbee in the woods. We had reasonable luck Picking up furs yesterday. I am on the St. Stephens And Koenton road. There is not much traveling this morning. The road is so bad. I am certainly Lomesome by myself not even my faithful little dog is with me it is 10 oclock A.M. The timber here is oak and Pine princiably. The beautiful Magnolias will soon be in Bloom. The bright and sunny Dixieland is certainly A pretty place All the year But springtime is the prettiest when all the timber is Leafing And the woods is full of flowers. Especcialy Grandpa grey beard it is A white feathery flower grows on trees along the swamps it looks like the trees is covered with snow. Everybody is busy plowing and planting now. Just think of our Northern Brothers is shivering with cold And will for nearly two months yet While we are eating vegatables that we have raised this spring. O I am sad this evening. O so sad[.] Papa Dear Papa has walked All day to find the mule. And now he is on his way home to see if she has gone there. I have had some Adventures with Wild animals scince I have been traveling But O this is the worst expericince I have ever stood To Kiss Dear Papa Goodbye And turn my face away while he walked out of sight of me Alone. God be with him and all till we meet again. The sun is shining bright this evening.

THURSDAY [MARCH] 13. . . . Well we passed A very comfortable night and next morning. Thank the Lord the rain has ceased to fall. Well I cooked breakfast and I sure hurried for the sky was still cloudy and the thunder was still rumbling in the south. Any one not used to the Pines is always thinking that A storm is coming on A Windy day They certainly roar. Well the forest fires has cleaned up all the dead grass and leaves and Pine needles. And the trees are in bloom and the oak are Just about full leafed and the pines certainly is A very pretty Back ground. The swamps in the spring is sure A pretty sight all kinds of flowers and vines and the evergreen certainly is pretty[.]

FRIDAY [MARCH] 14. . . . Well we are on our way home and Then for A jolly time my Friends. Well the Dogwoods are nearly in bloom then for the fishing Hooks and lines and Poles and bait cans. And Hurrah for the fish fries Just to talk about the fun then makes me wish I was on the creek pulling the finny beauties out of the water[.] Well the fur season will soon be over Then away to the Green fields and woods and the farm. I certainly love A farmers life better than A city life. For our city Brothers are so crowded and never get to enjoy the free country Life. . . .

**May Jordan** *was born in 1889 and died in 1914—just a year after these journal entries were written. Some of May's late entries tell of a decline in the quantity and quality of furs her father received; in fact, within just a few years many of the wild animals May describes in her journal were not very plentiful, if present at all, in the region. May's journal was saved by her family members and donated by her sister to the University of South Alabama Archives.*

# Rockefeller Wildlife Preserve: Mid-August

KEVIN MAHER

The air is moist
The water bittersweet
A southern Gulf breeze sighs
Laughing gulls call
And cicadas click their
Luminous song
I smell the death scent
Of beached gars
And see the dreamy haze
Of oil on water
Nearby an alligator stares
With tabby eyes
A great heron startles
From its marsh bed
Standing on the rip-rap,
I peer at the water
And slowly hoist
The turkey neck on string
A blue-point crab
Grips the bait
I slyly dip the net
A good two feet away
And scoop up the crustacean

Without warning
And drop it into a bucket
To meet many friends,
Gifts of the Mississippi,
The day has reached its climax
Animals sleep through the heat,
Hiding in the wax myrtles
A snowy egret,
White plumage glistening,
Glides into the Roseau cane.

**Kevin Maher** *lives in Lafayette, Louisiana. He wrote this poem when he was twelve years old and was a grand prize winner in the 2000 River of Words Poetry and Art contest.*

# Buried Christmas Tree

## Mary Dodson Wade

*Broad, sandy, and backed by fragile dunes, the beaches of the Gulf Coast are treasured by local residents who know them well.*

Miguel walked along the shore just above the waves. It was December, but the southerly breeze made it warm enough to tramp along barefoot. He watched his dog dart this way and that to avoid the rollers coming in. Sometimes the waves came up farther on the beach than usual, leaving a white froth. Willie barked at the swooshing sound the foam bubbles made.

Miguel turned around. His tracks went in a straight line, but Willie left zigzagged prints in the wet sand. A hermit crab skittered by.

Gulls on the beach ahead of him screeched and quarreled over some bits of trash. They scattered when he got too close but settled right back down to continue pecking at their treasure.

Just then a large wave ran up the beach. It caught Miguel by surprise and drenched Willie. The dog scampered to higher ground and shook the water out in a spray.

A second wave hit Miguel's foot. Loose sand slithered out from under his toes. He watched as the waves took the sand out. Then he whistled, "Come on, Willie."

Miguel waved to his friend, Mr. Beal, as he passed the man's weather-beaten store. The store hugged the shore above high tide. Its windows were filled with the hooks and fishing reels Mr. Beal rented to tourists. Moppie, Mr. Beal's calico cat, sat in the window watching everything that was going on.

Mr. Beal and Moppie lived in back of the store. Sometimes, when Miguel didn't have Willie with him, he'd stroke the cat's soft fur as he watched Mr. Beal cut up bait. Tourist boats used the bait when they took people deep-sea fishing in the Gulf of Mexico.

Mr. Beal was stringing colored lights along the nets and cork floats that draped the front of the store. "Christmas is coming," he said.

"Yeah," said Miguel. "I just wish it would snow."

"Not likely," said Mr. Beal. "Anyway, I like it warm. No snow for me. That's why I live here."

Miguel had to admit that it was nice to walk around without a coat during most of the winter. But when the wind came out of the north, it did get cold. Maybe, just maybe, it would get cold enough to snow sometime. He helped his friend with the last strand of lights and then set out for home.

As he passed the store after school the next day, Miguel noticed a Christmas tree propped up against the front. It was as tall as Mr. Beal. "You need help?" he asked.

"Sure."

"Where are you going to put it?" asked Miguel.

Mr. Beal pointed to a deep hole not far from the water.

Miguel was confused. "You're going to plant it? It can't grow. There aren't any roots. Anyway, the salt water will kill it."

Mr. Beal smiled. "That's okay," he said.

Miguel shrugged and helped the store owner carry the tree

to the hole. They dropped it down. By the time Mr. Beal packed sand around it, the tree was half buried. "Good," he said. Miguel wondered if his friend was all right.

He told his mother about it that night as he mashed avocado for the guacamole. "Hmm," she said, "that is odd." Mr. Beal's wife had died some years ago. Maybe, Miguel's mother thought, she ought to check on the elderly man.

The next day, Mr. Beal was waiting for Miguel. Together they decorated the tree, hanging corks from the branches and a string of shells for a garland. "Wish we had a starfish for the top," said Miguel. Instead they tied two sand dollars together over the tip.

They placed larger shells around the bottom of the tree. One was a huge conch with glassy-smooth, peachy-pink insides. Then Mr. Beal brought out a beautiful shell with distinctive dark streaks down its length. Miguel's eyes lit up. "That's a lightning whelk, right? We studied that in school."

Mr. Beal nodded. "The Texas state shell."

Miguel and Mr. Beal surveyed their work. Miguel had to admit the tree was different. And it was beautiful somehow, even without lights.

As the days went by, the tree began to turn brown, just as Miguel knew it would. But Mr. Beal didn't say a word until one day right before Christmas. "You want to earn some money?"

"Yeah!" said Miguel.

"I need some more Christmas trees."

"Are you going to put one inside?"

"No, they'll go over there with the other one," said Mr. Beal, pointing to the tree they'd planted. Now Miguel was really confused.

"I'll pay you fifty cents for every tree you bring me."

"It's a deal," said Miguel. "Nobody needs their trees after Christmas. But what good are they to you?"

Mr. Beal just smiled.

Miguel spent all week going from house to house asking his neighbors if he could pick up their tree after the family was through with it. Lots of people had artificial trees, and some people wanted to take theirs to the recycling place to be chipped into mulch. But at ten houses he got permission to come back for the tree.

Christmas dawned with warm sunshine. Miguel was disappointed about not having any snow, but he had fun flying a new airplane his mother had given him.

That afternoon Miguel and his mother walked over to Mr. Beal's store with a bag of oranges and some paper-thin cookies with sugar and cinnamon sprinkled on top. Miguel had a catnip toy for Moppie.

Mr. Beal thanked them and brought out a small square box with Miguel's name on it. Miguel tore off the colorful paper. Inside he found a water-filled globe with a beach "snow" scene. When he turned the globe over, tiny white specks stirred, then settled gently on shells and starfish. He shook it again and watched the flakes swirl.

"That's about as close to snow as we're going to get," said Mr. Beal.

"It's perfect," said Miguel, making the snow fly again.

Near the end of the holidays, Miguel began picking up the trees he'd been promised. One by one, he tied them to the back of his bicycle and dragged them to the holes Mr. Beal had dug. Together they set them in and filled the holes. It took several days, but finally there was a line of trees standing in a row. Miguel went home with five dollars in his pocket, but he still couldn't figure out why Mr. Beal wanted to plant old Christmas trees.

All that winter Miguel watched as the trees lost their needles and stood bare. When the spring rains came, he asked Mr. Beal how the trees were doing. "Fine," his friend answered. They didn't look any different to Miguel.

Then came a scorching summer. The sun beat down. Crowds came to the beach. Miguel's mother had to water her flowers every evening to keep them alive. Mr. Beal's trees were nothing but sticks and bare branches. Miguel couldn't help teasing his friend. "How're your trees doing?" he'd ask.

"Things are coming along just fine," his friend would answer. But when Miguel stopped to take a close look at them, the only thing he saw alive was some grass growing among the bare branches.

Weeks went by. Then one hot, sticky fall day, the morning news talked about Hurricane Franklin out in the Gulf. The weatherman couldn't predict where it might hit the coast.

Dark clouds followed Miguel to school that morning. A little while after lunch, the principal's voice came over the loudspeaker: "Hurricane Franklin has begun to move toward the Texas coast, and we're just out of the main path. All students are now dismissed. Walkers and bikers are to go home immediately. Bus students report to your pickup places."

Miguel pedaled home with gray clouds rolling overhead. The wind pushed him around fiercely. He was barely inside the back door when huge drops started falling.

His mother arrived home just as Miguel did and quickly turned on the TV. Pointing to swirling clouds on the map in front of him, the weatherman announced: "Residents on the wet side of the storm can expect ten to fifteen inches of rain. Beach erosion will occur along this area as storm surges carry away the sand."

"That means lots of rain for us," said his mother.

The wind got louder and the rain came down harder. Miguel worried about his friend. "I hope Mr. Beal is okay."

"That old store has been there quite a long time," said his mother. "I'm sure he's fine."

Miguel stared out at the rain. It raced down the street in huge swirling streams of water. The wind howled around the corner of the house. The stop sign on the corner was twisting in a frenzy, while the palm trees across the street stretched and bowed in a crazy dance. Miguel closed the drapes.

He was getting ready for bed when the lights went off. His mother lit a candle so he could finish brushing his teeth. He crawled into bed and pulled the covers over his ears. Even that did not keep out the noise of the wind and rain. It was a long time before he finally dropped off to sleep.

The next morning a shaft of sunlight awakened Miguel. He went outside into the clear cool air. The sky was a bright blue—so different from yesterday.

After breakfast, he pedaled down to Mr. Beal's store. Trash and seaweed lay far up on the beach. The waves were still fairly high.

"Things were really blowing last night," said Mr. Beal, "but we didn't get the full force of the hurricane."

"Yeah," said Miguel, "I was afraid something might happen to you."

"Oh, we made it fine," said his friend. "And come, I'll show you something."

They walked down to the row of trees they'd planted. Some of the sand had been carried away, but where grass had grown around the branches, most of the sand remained.

"Look," said Mr. Beal, "I'm growing a sand dune. It will be good for the beach and good for my store."

Miguel nodded, finally understanding why Mr. Beal had buried the Christmas trees. Then he ran down toward the beach and scooped up some dry sand. He brought back two fistfuls and scattered it over the bare limbs.

"What was that for?" asked Mr. Beal.

"Sand snow," said Miguel. "I think it's the only kind we're ever going to get."

**Mary Dodson Wade** *spent twenty-five years working as an elementary librarian before turning to full-time writing. She lives in Houston, Texas, with her husband, a consulting engineer. They enjoy traveling on his worldwide teaching assignments.*

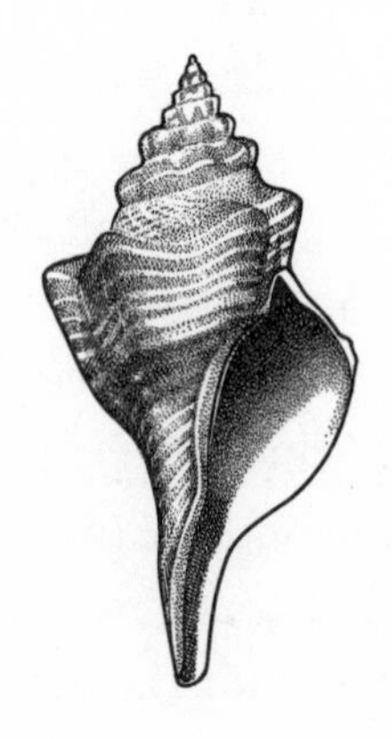

# Florida Haiku

## Mary Beth Lundgren

Powdery soft sugar sand
supports a streetlamp with an
osprey nest on top.

Thunder-black cloud looms
over orange tile roofs.
Egret and I sail toward home.

One side: sun, blue sky.
Clouds burst on the other.
A double rainbow arcs.

Black spider, big as
a baseball, spins a steel web
through scarlet milkweed.

**Mary Beth Lundgren,** *who has written for children for the last ten years, moved with her husband and two elderly cats from Cleveland, Ohio, to Cape Coral, Florida, in 1999. The strange beauty of her new Gulf Coast world constantly amazes her. In 2001, Henry Holt and Company published her newest book,* Love, Sara, *a teen novel in which the main character writes, among other things, poetry.*

# Winter Texans in Aransas

Virginia E. Parker-Staat

*In 1941, only 21 whooping cranes lived in the wild, and fifteen of them wintered in Texas. Now protected in both their Canada nesting grounds and their Texas winter home, the whoopers are making a comeback. By the 1999–2000 winter, a record 188 whooping cranes visited Texas's Aransas National Wildlife Refuge. Their success is a tribute to the cranes' will to survive and the people working to protect the whoopers' home.*

## The Arrival

When the breeze along the Texas coast begins to chill, skyways fill with the sounds of birds. Brisk north winds bring arrow-patterned clouds of Canada geese. Their chorus of honking marks the beginning of a grand migration. Hundreds of thousands of birds flock to the Texas coast, including the most famous of winter Texans, the magnificent whooping crane.

Whooping cranes migrate to Texas each winter. They fly more than 2,400 miles from Wood Buffalo National Park in Canada. Traveling with young chicks who have only a few weeks of flying experience, a family of whoopers may take three months to complete their journey. They stop for days or weeks along the Platte River in Nebraska. They may stop again in Kansas and Oklahoma to rest and feed. Finally they reach Texas, filling the air with their trumpeting territorial calls.

As November approached when I was a child, those first sounds of geese honking and cranes trumpeting stirred something wild within me. I would dash across the pasture with my arms outstretched, the wind tugging at my hair, wishing I could somehow take flight. I wanted to be the first bird, the one that led the entire flock across Goose Island, past the thousand-year-old live oak known as Big Tree, and on to Aransas Bay.

Today, bird-watchers continue to gather at the Aransas National Wildlife Refuge near Austwell, Texas. With binoculars and cameras ready, birders search the skies. Whoopers have become the most anxiously awaited arrivals to the shores of Blackjack Peninsula.

By early November, the forty-foot observation tower at Aransas crowds with visitors. A stir begins whenever large birds come into view. Voices buzz. Which whooper family will arrive first? How many chicks survived the long flight? Has the flock increased its numbers?

Lucky birders finally see their reward. Overhead flies a huge white crane, with black wing tips that are only visible when it's flying. Whoopers arrive in small numbers, normally family groups. They fly with their necks and feet outstretched.

Standing nearly five feet tall and weighing about fifteen pounds, whooping cranes are the tallest and heaviest of North America's wading birds. Their nearly eight-foot wing span stretches longer than most doorways are tall. Many refer to the birds as whoopers because of their deep, organlike call.

Whoopers have bright yellow eyes. Their strong, dark-olive

gray beaks extend more than six inches. They sport a patch of red skin with no feathers on their heads. Their feet are not webbed, allowing them to spread three large toes and wade in shallow shores.

On their arrival at Aransas, the cranes' enormous wing tips skim the water. Each whooper family reclaims the same territory every year. They spend each winter in Aransas's tidal flats, a fringe of ground where sea and land meet.

## Life on the Flats

The rippling tidal flats offer a perfect winter home for whoopers. Southeasterly winds drive seawater into bays and tidal flats. Northwesterly winds blow the water out to sea. The water constantly changes from very salty to brackish, depending on rain and tidal flow.

A variety of plants and animals lives in this odd environment. Wispy cordgrass and patches of sea ox-eye provide safety for marine life. Bright green algal mats clump along the grasses, bobbing with the tides. Crimson red wolfberries mix with knee-high marsh elder. Flower clusters of marsh fleabane dust the flats in shades of violet.

Whooping cranes wade the tidal flats, poking and jabbing for food. They enjoy eating blue crabs, mud shrimp, frogs, crayfish, and clams. Occasionally they feed on berries and grains.

The cranes spend most of their day feeding. The remainder of the time, they rest, preen feathers, and squabble among themselves over territory. Occasionally their whoops and calls signal approaching predators. When they sleep, they usually stand with one leg raised.

## The Aransas Community

Whoopers share Aransas National Wildlife Refuge with more than 400 other species of birds, including herons, egrets, ducks, and geese. Aransas is also home to several other endangered birds, including brown pelicans, peregrine falcons, and wood storks.

Aransas is the oldest coastal preserve in Texas. Established in 1937 to protect whooping cranes and other migratory waterfowl, the 55,563-acre refuge boasts tidal flats, marshes, ponds, grasslands, and thickets.

Aransas fills the senses. On warm mornings, the sounds of singing insects combine with the squawking of gulls, croaking of frogs, and buzzing of bees. Dew-laced spiderwebs glisten in the sunlight and billow like sails in the constant breeze. The wind rustles through crackling dry reeds. Nearby blackjack and live oak thickets soften gusts to gentle sighs.

In the tidal flat and marsh, the sludgelike soil can tug tennis shoes off feet. The sticky goo reeks with the smell of decaying plants. Restless tides lap at the ever changing shoreline.

Moving inland, the soil changes to deep sand. Refuge trails reveal tracks of the abundant but shy wildlife. White-tailed deer leave two-pronged points in the silty sand. Opossum leave starlike marks. Raccoons leave babylike handprints.

Sharp-eyed visitors may spot bristly javelina rooting for acorns. Alligators bask in shallow waters, the crowns of their heads and eyes barely breaking the surface. Distant flocks of Canada geese look like snow on grassy meadows. Rarely seen predators such as coyotes and bobcats prowl for food.

Life moves more rhythmically along the coastal bend, away from bustling cities. The sun and moon tug, making the tides

rise and fall. Gulf breezes add moisture to the air, lending a painter's palette of colors at dawn and dusk. Trees along the Texas coast lean gracefully in the direction of prevailing winds.

Changing seasons are signaled by the direction of winds and the flight of birds. By autumn, when the geese and cranes come home, everyone welcomes the chill in the winds that bring them.

## Winter to Spring . . . to Winter

During a Texas winter, all creatures constantly watch for the charcoal-gray clouds that signal damp and chilling winds called Northers. With no mountains and few trees to slow cold fronts, temperatures can drop twenty degrees in a matter of minutes.

After the chill of Canada's springs, whooping cranes take Texas winters calmly. Their feathers may ruffle in blustery winds, but they rarely leave their tidal flats for warmer grounds. Whoopers normally fly inland only when the water turns too salty and they must find fresh water for drinking.

By early spring, Aransas vibrates with a new energy and whoopers begin their amazing dance. To court their mates, they fluff their feathers and stomp their pencil-thin legs and feet. They wave and bow their red-crowned heads. Like stiff ballerinas, they leap peg-legged into the air.

Soon their mate begins to mimic the leaps and bows. Within moments, the two birds point their heads upward. They begin to whoop and sing in unison. Sometimes other cranes join the wild song and strange dance.

In March or early April, the cranes become restless. Soon they return to their nesting grounds in Canada, often making the journey in only two weeks. They weave enormous nests from rush and grass. Female whoopers lay two pale green eggs with olive-colored specks. Both parents take turns nesting until their chicks hatch. In less than three months, the chicks test their wings for flight.

When September's frosty fingers turn Canada's leaves to gold, whoopers long for the shores of Aransas Bay. With their new families, they take a half-dozen leaping strides and flap their giant wings. With rapid upstrokes, they join another grand migration of birds heading south. Using steady wing-beats, the whoopers fly once again to the warm waters of their Texas winter home.

**Virginia E. Parker-Staat** *has written fourteen children's books and a variety of educational passages and short stories. She is a sixth-generation Texan, now living near Houston with her husband, David. They have grown twin sons. She travels often, returning to visit and write about the wilder corners of the Texas coast and beyond.*

Reapers and Sowers

# My First Dog

I. C. Eason

*as told to Blair Pittman*

*I. C. Eason spent his entire life in the swampy wildlands of the Neches River Bottom in East Texas. Residents of this area were known as the Dog People because they hunted for food just as their ancestors did—using dogs to track razorback hogs, deer, panthers, and bears. In the early 1970s, I. C. Eason recounted this story of his first dog to a visiting photographer named Blair Pittman.*

One Saturday night, late, about nine or ten o'clock, my little brother Deacon and me come walking home from the river bottom totin' our game. We'd been huntin' and fishin', getting us somethin' to eat for the week. The kerosene lamp was still burnin' and Mama and Daddy was waitin' up for us. The light shined out the window onto the porch and we was looking at the squirrels and fish we had.

We was about to take it all in the house to show them when I seen somethin'. I thought I seen somethin' move. There was somethin' black layin' in the corner of the yard.

Deacon, who was littler than me, was scairt. He wanted to go on in the house but I told him to get some pine splinters for a torch. He got it lit and we eased in for a closer look. It was a dog and his tail was a-waggin'. Boy, then I seen it–blood was all over him. He didn't growl none, didn't make a sound. He just kept on a-waggin' his tail, tellin' me it was all right.

Deacon held the splinter torch in closer so I could see better. His head wasn't bloody. I moved my hand, real slow, and patted him behind the head. A hurt dog like this could be dangerous but he still didn't make a sound. That tail just wagged. His foreleg was almost cut off, just barely hanging, and his belly was cut from front to back. His guts was stickin' out in a knot, the size of both my fists. Only thing I could think of that could do that much damage was a razorback hog. I'd even heard about one big boar that picked up a horse and rider and cut both of them up real bad.

He wasn't wearin' no collar so there was no way to tell where he was from or who he belonged to. I don't know why he happened to pick our yard, but here he was. When I moved my hand close to his mouth, he sniffed it, then licked my hand. I knew right then that I wanted that dog.

In the house I went. I told Mama and Daddy I'd found a hurt dog and I needed a pan of water and a clean rag. Mama tore a piece off an old sheet for me while I dipped water in a dishpan. Then they come outside to have a look for themselves.

I started cleaning him, real easy like. Lordy, you couldn't tell just how much he was hurt because the blood was caked all over him. Daddy brought out the lamp and held it up for a good look. He shook his head, no, then handed the lamp over to Deacon. Daddy stomped back into the house mutterin' about how crazy kids was, that the best thing to do was knock that dog in the head with a hammer. I didn't listen to him. I just kept cleanin' and the dog's tail just kept on a-waggin'. Mama knowed about hurt things, so she stayed to see if she could help.

The caked-on blood was getting soft. I kept on wiping and

wringing out the rag till I finally got him clean enough I could see old scars. This dog had been cut before. There wasn't no doubt this was a hog dog and probably a good one too. Boy, those guts sticking out had dirt on them. That just wouldn't do. If he was gonna live, they had to be cleaned and sewed up. I didn't like the idea of washin' his guts, but they had to be put back in.

Mama went to the house for a needle. We didn't have no thread so she used string from flour sacks for sewing clothes. That would have to do for the dog.

I started sewing up his leg. That wasn't too bad. I was talking to him, kind of quiet-like. Ever so often, his tail would wag. Then I got to his belly. He must of licked on hisself some because some of the fat was gone. Anyway, I washed his guts off the best I could and stuck them back in. I sewed him up just like Mama would sew a pair of pants. I overlapped the skin and started stitchin', over and under, over and under, tyin' off each stitch as I went. When I was finished, Deacon and I lifted him, gentle-like, and laid him on the porch. Then we sat there with him for a while, pettin' and talkin'.

He was pretty—mostly black but his belly was white. Down the inside of three legs was white, three of his feet was white and he had a white ring around his neck. There wasn't no other name for him but Ring. We covered him with a towsack and told him goodnight.

The next mornin' I was up early. Ring was layin' on the front porch just like I'd left him. I wasn't sure he was alive. Then I saw his tail wag and he started trying to get up. I went over and pushed him down. I didn't want those stitches popping loose.

We just barely had enough food for us. None to spare. I went out to the corn crib, got an ear of corn, put it in a sack and beat it to cornmeal with a hammer. I poured some water in the meal and baked it for him, just like he was somebody. Whatever we had to eat, that's what Ring had to eat. He ate whether I ate or not. I fed him the best I could.

In a couple of weeks, Ring was lookin' good. He was walking some, stiff-like, getting his strength back and startin' to get fat eatin' up everything I could bring him. In another week, he was gettin' around almost as good as new.

When I got up in the mornings, that's when Ring got up. He started goin' with me while I was workin'. He'd sit and watch while I plowed. Ever now and then, he'd follow me up a row, then stop and wait for me to make another round. I guess he was exercising. By then, we had two mules for plowin', a big one and a little one. The big one was kind of a blue color so that's what we called her—Blue. The first thing I had to do every morning was catch them. The younger mule would do whatever Blue done. I don't even recollect the other one's name. But boy, I remember Blue.

We'd turn them out every evenin'. Back then, there wasn't no stock laws and not many fences, so the mules could wander pretty far. Then next mornin' it was my job to find them. Well, Blue got to where she didn't want to get caught. We kept a long rope tied around her neck so we could grab her, but it was always a devil of a time. Blue was good at knowin' how fast and how far to move to keep me from gettin' the end of the draggin' rope. Damn, that mule thought she was smart. She'd priss around, eatin' grass, but watchin' me all the time. I'll tell you one thing, once she was caught, that was fine. There wasn't no better mule for plowin' in the country. You could even plow her without a bridle—but she had to be caught first.

The first time I knowed Ring was good for anything was

when he went with me to catch Blue. Ring just kind of followed me around like a puppy dog. Of course, Blue wanted to play hard to get. I'd ease up towards her, gettin' closer and closer to the end of the rope. Just about when I was ready to dive for it, off she'd go, just out of reach. If I'd run fast, she'd move just that much faster. Ring didn't seem interested in all this. He just stayed right beside me, watchin'. I made another run at the mule. And then, somethin' happened. I just stopped, mad as I could be. I didn't even think. I just turned to Ring and said, "Get 'er, Ring." That's all I had to say. He was gone and so was the mule. Side by side runnin' full gallop, Ring pulled in beside her front shoulder. Then he jumped, grabbed her nose and pulled her head down between the front legs and turned her a flip. KA-WHUMP! She hit the ground on her back. Ring knowed when to let go. He stepped back and stood there watchin'.

Blue got up and looked at Ring, her eyes buggin' out. The damned mule took off again, kickin' and buckin'. Ring looked back at me and I said, "Get 'er again, Ring." Off he went, caught up to her and, KA-WHUMP, did it again.

After the third time, Blue didn't get up. I thought she had a broke neck but she just had the wind knocked out of her. She didn't get up till I picked up the rope. Then she stood there, kind of quiverin' all over. She seemed downright relieved to plow that day.

Every day, that's how it went. I'd be up just about the crack of daylight. I'd build a fire so Mama could cook breakfast. Then I'd go out on the front porch and there'd be Ring watchin' me with his head on his front feet. He'd raise up like he was askin' what I wanted him to do. If I needed to plow, I'd say, "Go get 'em, Ring." Quick as a shot he was gone. Them mules could be a mile and a half away, way down by the swamp, but it never took him more than fifteen minutes. You could hear 'em comin'. As long as the mules headed straight for the house, he never touched 'em. But if one turned, like they was goin' somewhere else, that was it, son. He'd bust that butt. Ring didn't give no trouble unless they asked for it.

I was proud of that dog. Ring was smart, all right, but knowin' how to catch a mule was just the first of it. He knowed how to hunt, too. Some dogs are good hunters but when they catch what they're after, they'll chew on it, maybe kill it before you can get there. Sometimes you can hardly break a dog of that. It's like somethin' wild in 'em—they try to kill whatever it is, a deer, a hog, or a cow. But Ring wasn't like that, never was. And he could hunt anything you'd tell him.

If I wanted a hog, I'd just tell him, "SOOOIE, Ring," and he was gone. He'd "yow, yow, yow" just often enough for me to know where he was. I could tell by listenin' to him. He'd change pitch when he got on a trail. It was just like he was talkin' to me. He got another sound in his voice when he caught up to 'em. I didn't have to hurry neither. When I got there, they was bayed. It didn't matter if it was one hog or ten, he held 'em, kept 'em circlin'. One would charge him and he'd back up just enough to get out of the way. Then he'd run him back into the circle. Oh, he'd nip at one every now and then, but he never brought blood.

When I'd get there, I'd pick out the hog I wanted, point him, and say, "That one, Ring." Shoot, it didn't matter whether he weighed two pounds or 200, that's the one he'd single out. The rest of 'em could go, but that one was staying. He could try the best he knowed to get back in the bunch but he couldn't. Ring was always there to cut him off. Finally, the hog would hold his ground and paw at the dirt, chomp his teeth, and wave his tusks, but that was a whipped hog, outsmarted by Ring. Shoot! I didn't even need a gun. I'd just carry a claw hammer with me. While Ring kept the hog busy, I'd get in there and knock him in the head.

Ring was just as good with deer too. That's a whole different way of huntin'. Ring and I got so good at deer, once he picked up a trail and let out his "yow, yow, yow," that deer was as good as dead.

It didn't work for anyone to hunt with Ring but me. Most folks might shoot two, three, or four times. Ring learned that once he brought a deer close to me, one shot and the hunt was over. Ring would quit the hunt. I couldn't shoot but once because I didn't have but a single-barrel shotgun.

That dog meant a lot to me and to my brothers and sisters. He meant food on the table. Without him, we would have been hungry. I didn't hunt him for nothin'. When we went into the woods, it didn't take all day neither. Hog, deer, squirrel, whatever I hunted, that's just what we come back to the house with.

For a little over a year, that's how it went. Then one day, a man come ridin' to the house and talked to Daddy. The man started describin' a dog he'd lost last year in a hog hunt. He wanted to know if we had seen a dog like that.

I stood behind the door and listened. Daddy being a preacher—a good Christian, you know—allowed as how we'd found a dog like that. Daddy went on to tell the man how bad hurt the dog had been. He told the man how his boy had sewed up his dog and made it well. The man said he was beholden for takin' such good care of his dog. Daddy whistled and here come Ring. The man looked him over, nodded his head yep, and said, "This sure is my dog." He tied a lariat rope around his neck, got on his horse, and was leadin' Ring away, ridin' off down the road.

That was all I could take. I busted out the front door, big old tears runnin' down my face, and ran down the road after them. I caught up to him and the man stopped. I looked back at the house. Daddy was standin' on the porch, watchin', but he was out of earshot. "Mister," I told him, "you're a dirty son-of-a—." He just turned around and kept on ridin', with Ring lookin' back at me from the end of the rope.

Well, that man got to the top of the hill, 100 yards or so away, and stopped his horse. He got off and untied Ring. He hollered to me. "Boy, if this here dog will come to you, he's yours."

All I had to say was, "Here, Ring." He pulled away from the man and here he come runnin' as fast as he could. The man tried to call him, but Ring didn't even look back.

And that's how I got my first dog.

*The Dog People of East Texas lived with almost no contact with the outside world until the 1970s, when environmentalists, timber companies, oil companies, and the federal government entered into a debate about how best to use the lands they'd lived off for centuries.* **I. C. Eason,** *with his extraordinary knowledge of and devotion to the forests, became the Dog People's spokesman. While wary of all the groups, he had the least objection to the environmentalists and their interests. In 1974, President Gerald Ford created the 84,500-acre Big Thicket National Preserve on much of the Dog People's land.*

# Port O'Connor 9/1/99

JERRY WERMUND

The gentle cold front passes,
ineffective in altering
hot summer ground.
All is still,
hot-sticky still.
Above,
puffy clouds hang
anchored,
immobile,
growing taller,
seized by updrafts
off the baking earth—
a reflector oven.
We on the ground pray for
clouds in the air, yearn for
any favor from wind
any side current
any lateral puff.

**Jerry Wermund** *is a retired professional geologist who now writes for children from his home in the Hill Country of Texas. An avid nature lover, he enjoys sharing his vision of the natural world that he has explored over a long career outdoors. Coastal regions are among his favored landscapes.*

# Remembering Bull Run Road

SHELLIE RUSHING TOMLINSON

*Imported by the first colonists, cotton soon found the perfect growing conditions in a broad belt of fertile soil that stretches across the southern United States. Since that time, cotton has come to define the economy, social structure, and culture of many Gulf Coast communities, including the Louisiana farm region where Shellie Rushing Tomlinson was raised.*

I grew up on Bull Run Road in a little cluster of farming families called Melbourne Community, right in the heart of the Louisiana Delta. Our corner of the world was just a bump on a stretch of Highway 65 between Tallulah and Lake Providence. Almost everyone in our community farmed, except for the family running the local grocery and the preacher's family at the Baptist church. Farming shaped our community. An old Southern expression dating back to the 1800s says it best: "Cotton is King." From an early age my sisters and I understood that our family's lives on the farm revolved around the cotton and its long growing season.

Each year the first hint of spring signaled the beginning of the cotton season, and the community would begin to buzz with activity as farmers prepared the land and equipment for planting. At the same time, in stubborn opposition to the farmers' plans, the spring rains would begin to fall steadily, bringing with them the threat of flooding. Parallel to Highway 65 ran a long, high, snakelike mound of dirt, a man-made levee system that struggled each spring to keep the mighty Mississippi River from overflowing its banks and swallowing us whole. The Corps of Engineers staged a continual battle with Old Man River, working around the clock to bring in tons of dirt and hundreds of sandbags. As they struggled to strengthen the levee's walls, the churning river chiseled relentlessly at its sides from within. We lived with the constant threat of a flood. For weeks the adults would talk of nothing else until one day the spring rains would stop abruptly as if someone had turned off a huge water faucet. A couple of short months later when summer settled in and one-hundred-degree temperatures baked their thirsty young crops, the farmers would hold their hats in one hand and scratch their heads with the other as they searched the skies and prayed for rain.

During these early months of the growing season, while the crops were young and the days were growing longer, my sisters and I embraced the large blocks of free time we had each afternoon after school. Our farm was like one giant adventure land and we never grew tired of exploring it. My sisters and I were an early version of latchkey kids. If the weather was pretty Mama locked the latch and we played outside. She had a lot of cooking and cleaning to do and we weren't going to be underfoot. Poor Mama, she was a true Southern lady. She was crowned Miss Forestry Queen as a teenager living in Natchez, Mississippi. She deserved at least one proper little girl—someone who liked to dress up and play tea party. Instead she got Cyndie, Rhonda, and Shellie, three dyed-in-the-wool tomboys.

One of our favorite games was chase-don't-touch-the-ground. Like everything else we did on Bull Run Road, it wasn't a game for the faint-hearted. Papa's tractor shed was the playing field. We jumped from tractor to combine, swung from rafter to rafter, slid down poles, and crawled over the two-story tin roof—anything to avoid the chaser who was . . . jumping from tractor to combine, swinging from rafter to rafter, and sliding down poles to get to be the chasee. Sometimes in our haste we did end up hitting the ground—hard!

We invented another game that was just as much fun and just as likely to end badly. This time Papa's shed was a great racetrack, carved out around the heavy farm equipment. The players were on bicycles, and there was only one way for the chaser to get to be the chasee—knock someone down. It wasn't enough to touch her bike; she had to crash.

Spring was also a good time to go crawdad fishing. Crawdads lived in the shallow water of drainage ditches that ran beneath the rusty bridges dotting the roads of Melbourne Community. The fishing was easy. A ball of twine confiscated from Papa's tractor shed, a kitchen knife (Mama's scissors worked better, but taking 'em was costly), and the fishing was on. My sisters and I would cut a length of string and tie a piece of bacon on the end. Crawdads loved bacon! You could watch their little pinchers close around it if the water wasn't muddy from too much rain. And if it was muddy, you just waited for the nudge the old crawdad would give you. The trick was to jerk the string up and over your head so the crawdad would smack the road and lie stunned long enough for you to avoid his pinchers and pick him up. Crawdads are aggressive little creatures. We liked to watch them rear back on their tails and wave their pinchers around wildly. They looked like miniature versions of the animated dinosaurs we saw on Saturday morning cartoons. Another distinguishing characteristic of the crawdads is their strong odor. They smell bad—like the worst fish you've ever smelled, times two. Even the black gumbo mud beneath the bridge took on their odor.

One day Cyndie, Rhonda, and I were fishing a little piece from the house when a neighbor girl came cruising by on her new bike. We tried to hide our envy with indifference while she pedaled back and forth on the bridge.

Neighbor Girl's bike had the latest braking system. Instead of the brakes being on the pedals, they were on the handlebars. If you hit those foot pedals to stop, like we were all accustomed to, you weren't stopping and you were likely to skin your bare toe on the road when your foot slipped off.

On her last fly by, Neighbor Girl intended to skid to the rail and stop to see how the fishing was going, or maybe she wanted to taunt us one more time. Trouble was, she forgot about the new brakes and hit her foot pedals instead. She went into a free fall—bike and all—right over the rail and into the water. It wasn't a long fall, and the water couldn't have been more than a couple of feet deep. But it gave us plenty of reason to hoot and holler all the way home.

By the time school let out for the summer, the long days and hot weather had spurred the young cotton plants to maturity. They would be four to five feet high and overlapping in the middle with unwanted weeds rising up, threatening to choke them. Mama might've missed having little ladies but if Papa missed having a son, we never knew it. He took his three tomboys and showed us the value of a hard day's work, paying us a dollar an hour to hoe the cotton. Mama would wake us for a big breakfast while Papa sharpened the hoes for the day's chopping. A hoe is a long farm implement that looks like a shovel but with a flat sharp edge. Outside the house a truckload of laborers would be waiting to work the fields with us. We were a multiracial group bound by need—theirs to earn a dollar and Papa's to teach his girls a work ethic he knew would benefit us the rest of our lives.

In the mornings the cotton would be wet with dew, and the plants were almost over our heads. This meant our clothes got wet right off. Although no one liked getting drenched so early, we learned that everything was relative when the sun climbed high in the sky and beat down on us unmercifully. Our job was to walk a row of cotton plants looking for offending grasses like Johnson grass or cuckleburrows. These hardy trespassers have to go. If the weeds are allowed to remain mixed in with the cotton, they lower the price the farmer can get for his crop. When we found the unwanted grass we chopped it down with our hoe, being careful to avoid damaging the precious plants.

As the day wore on, the rows seemed to grow longer. The water coolers waiting to quench our thirst at the end of the rows seemed to get farther and farther away. So we invented imaginative ways to cover the ground. As novices, we plodded along tending to one row each. With experience we learned a really good hand could walk in the center of one row while monitoring neighboring rows at the same time. Papa was the final judge on who was a novice and who could handle more than one row.

Sometimes things livened up quickly if someone happened upon a snake. There are many poisonous and nonpoisonous snakes in Louisiana. The cottonmouth, rattlesnake, and water moccasin are a few of the dangerous snakes that shared our Delta. We were taught to recognize them from an early age. We learned that a snake is a poor opponent for a sharp hoe.

Hoeing was hard work, but there were a few perks for Papa's girls. If we were working close to the house, Papa would take us home early for lunch so we could watch our favorite show, *The Young and the Restless.* Mama usually had a big meal ready, and if she didn't, she had thick slices of bologna from the country store. When I hear the word "bologna," I don't think of the thin almost odorless slices you find in a supermarket. I think of stiff white paper folded around chunky slices of pure heaven, each slice of meat encircled with its own red wrapper.

We complained about hoeing, of course, but I'll never forget the pride I felt on payday when Papa would come home with a whole stack of one-dollar bills and count out our hours.

Delta summers are long, hot, and dry and they only begin to end when you can't remember anything else. One morning you wake up and the air smells different, cleaner somehow, and nips at your bare arms. The days begin to shorten and all signs point to the harvest. That's when the farmers roll out their cottonpickers and combines, blow them off, oil them up, and unleash them on the heavily laden fields.

By this time we were back in school, but Papa would let us pack cotton for him in the evening when we got home. We were in our rooms almost before the bus could roll to a stop, racing to change into play clothes and meet Papa in the field. The closer we got to the tall cotton trailers, the stronger the familiar smells became. Even now, it's hard for me to distinguish between the strong woodsy smell of cotton in my memory and the bitter smell of stinkbugs. These little green bugs leave a disagreeable odor wherever they walk. If you fool around and squash a stinkbug, the smell intensifies. Because stinkbugs love cotton, the two are inseparable at harvesttime.

When the bin on the cottonpicker filled up, Papa would dump his load of white, fluffy cotton into the trailer and ramble off quickly so the monster machine could eat up as much as possible before the sun began its descent and the rising moisture signaled the day's end. Meanwhile, Cyndie, Rhonda, and I would stay in the trailer to stomp the cotton.

There are at least two ways to stomp, or pack, cotton, but only one purpose—to allow more cotton into the trailer and thus have fewer trips to the cotton gin, which speeds up the harvest. The adult labor stomped around in a slow, methodical pattern until the cotton was conquered. Our way was much more fun. We'd climb onto the sides of the trailer and jump, dive, and fall into the white stuff over and over. In this raw state, cotton isn't all soft and cuddly. Instead, it's strewn with the scratchy brown husks that once held the individual cotton bolls on the plant. We wore blue jeans and long sleeves when we packed to avoid the itchy scrapes of these husks. While we played we were obligated to keep an eye out for Papa. If his cottonpicker were close to filling up again, we went into serious stomping mode so as not to slow him down when he came around to dump another load.

We loved to dig tunnels in the cotton. We were experts at packing and forming the stretchy white stuff into a maze of tunnels beneath the visible top layer. The tunnels scared Papa and Mama and were only allowed under certain conditions. You could never, ever play in the cotton by yourself, and you could never under any circumstances dig tunnels while the trailer was in the field. Mama had known a little boy who fell asleep and suffocated in his bed of cotton because his dad dumped a fresh load on him without knowing he was there. Only when Papa stored a trailer overnight under the shed could we create our white wonderland.

There is a small window of opportunity to harvest a crop and sometimes haste would edge out caution and we would hear of someone losing a finger or hand to the big machinery. Just about everyone knew someone who had been maimed or killed in a harvest-related incident. Sometimes a load of cotton would begin to smolder, bursting into flames in the steel bin of the cottonpicker while the unsuspecting driver continued down the field.

I remember my own harvest accident. We'd been playing hard for hours, and I was taking a breather, perched on the top of the cotton trailer. I lost my balance and fell backward onto the hard-packed road. Cyndie and Rhonda climbed down quickly, sure I was dead or dying. They only began to laugh once the breath came back into my body and they felt confident I would live.

Once the crops were harvested it was time to plow the fields before they were left vacant for the winter months. Cyndie learned to drive a tractor early, a skill Rhonda and I nearly avoided. Then one day I took a crash course.

Papa was just finishing some maintenance on his tractor when I happened by. He caught a quick glimpse of me.

"Cyndie," he said, "get on this tractor and follow me around the shed and help me hook up to the planter."

I tried to explain that I wasn't Cyndie but he cut me off gruffly and stormed in the direction of the shed. Given the opportunity I would have explained that I didn't know how to drive a tractor. Instead I climbed aboard and looked around. I'd ridden with Papa enough to know how to crank it up. I even managed to follow him in first gear. I was feeling pretty pleased with myself. But my pleasure was short-lived.

As we pulled up beside the shed, Papa hollered at me to stop. Unfortunately, this was the first time I looked for the brake. I found two of them! Did I know the left brake stopped the left wheel and the right brake the right wheel and unless you pressed them both the tractor would take a hard turn in the direction of whichever one you chose? No! I simply chose the one on the left and hit it hard. Unfortunately, that was the same side the shed was on.

One loud crash later, I held my breath and met Papa's surprised eyes. He chuckled. "Shellie Charlene," he asked, holding his side and laughing, "what are you doing up there? You don't know how to drive a tractor!" He took the words right out of my mouth.

After the crops were all harvested, the heavy machinery was cleaned and oiled and parked for the winter. With school in full swing and the holidays fast approaching, cotton faded into the background of our lives while my sisters and I dreamed of Christmas and tried to stay off Santa's naughty list.

Louisiana winters are short and mild, with stretches of chilly weather broken here and there by short bursts of freezing temperatures. But before we knew it the sun would start to warm the land and the eternal tension between King Cotton's impatience and Mother Nature's spring rains would return once again to take center stage of our lives.

**Shellie Rushing Tomlinson** *is a farmer's wife, mother, interior designer, and girls' basketball coach. She currently lives with her husband and teenagers in Lake Providence, Louisiana. Her parents survived their daughters' childhood and teenage years and still live on the family farm.*

# Mollie Tree

REESE DANLEY-KILGO

It was a name that suited her.
She was tall, and straight, held her head
high. She walked firmly, but lightly
on the Alabama land she loved, had lived
on, for almost eighty years.

Tightly she holds my hand in hers
as we walk, my grandmother and I,
past the pasture, by the barn,
through the field, down the hill.

It is June. Everything is summer green.
I am ten. I have been here every summer
of my life.

Summer solstice, she says.
The lightest, longest day. When it is done,
the sun will turn. This is the day,
if we sit quietly here, we will hear
birdsong
you will remember all of your life.

All the songs the birds have ever sung
are still here, in the leaves
of these trees. They can be heard again,
on this one day of summer, if you listen
long enough, if you sit here quiet enough.

I remember, Mollie Tree. I remember
you and me, walking, sitting on the bank
of the Choctahatchee River, in the cool
green shade, on the lightest, longest
day of the year, of the summer
when I was ten.

*A teacher and counselor for many years,* **Reese Danley-Kilgo** *is now a writer and a gardener. Her most recent book of poems is* Poems Since Salamander. *She lives in Huntsville, Alabama.*

# The Alligator and the Hunter

*A Choctaw Story*

JOSEPH BRUCHAC

*The inhabitants of the Gulf Coast have long hunted animals for food and other necessities. To ensure that the hunters of today don't deprive the hunters of tomorrow, many communities have developed a code of ethics that governs hunters' practices. This story from the Choctaw Indians of Mississippi reveals very specific beliefs about the responsible way to hunt deer.*

There once was a man who had very bad luck when he hunted. Although the other hunters in his village were always able to bring home deer, this man never succeeded. He was the strongest of the men in the village and he knew the forest well, but his luck was never good. Each time he came close to the deer, something bad would happen. A jay would call from the trees and the deer would take flight. He would step on dry leaves and the deer would run before he could shoot. His arrow would glance off a twig and miss the deer. It seemed there was no end to his troubles. Finally the man decided he would go deep into the swamps where there were many deer. He would continue hunting until he either succeeded or lost his own life.

The man hunted for three days without success. At noon on the fourth day, he came to a place in the swamp where there had once been a deep pool. The late summer had been a very dry one, however, and now there was only hot sand where once there had been water. There, resting on the sand, was a huge alligator. It had been without water for many days. It was so dry and weak that it was almost dead. Although the hunter's own luck had been bad, he saw that this alligator's luck was even worse.

"My brother," said the man, "I pity you."

Then the alligator spoke. Its voice was so weak that the man could barely hear it. "Is there water nearby?" said the alligator.

"Yes," said the man. "There is a deep pool of clear cool water not far from here. It is just beyond that small stand of trees to the west. There the springs never dry up and the water always runs. If you go to that place, you will survive."

"I cannot travel there by myself," said the alligator. "I am too weak. Come close so I can talk to you. I will not harm you. Help me and I will also help you."

The hunter was afraid of the great alligator, but he came a bit closer. As soon as he was close, the alligator spoke again.

"I know that you are a hunter but the deer always escape from you. If you help me, I will make you a great hunter. I will give you the power to kill many deer."

This sounded good to the hunter, but he still feared the alligator's great jaws. "My brother," the man said, "I believe that you will help me, but you are still an

alligator. I will carry you to that place, but you must allow me to bind your legs and bind your jaws so that you can do me no harm."

Immediately the alligator rolled over to its back and held up its legs. "Do as you wish," the alligator said.

The man bound the alligator's jaws firmly with his sash. He made a bark strap and bound the alligator's legs together. Then, with his great strength, he lifted the big alligator to his shoulders and carried it to the deep cool water where the springs never dried. He placed the alligator on its back close to the water and he untied its feet. He untied the alligator's jaws, but still held those jaws together with one hand. Then he jumped back quickly. The alligator rolled into the pool and dove underwater. It stayed under a long time and then came up. Three more times the alligator dove, staying down longer each time. At last it came to the surface and floated there, looking up at the hunter who was seated high on the bank.

"You have done as you said you would," said the alligator. "You have saved me. Now I shall help you, also. Listen closely to me now and you will become a great hunter. Go now into the woods with your bow and arrows. Soon you will meet a small doe. That doe has not yet grown large enough to have young ones. Do not kill that deer. Only greet it and then continue on and your power as a hunter will increase. Soon after that you will meet a large doe. That doe has fawns and will continue to have young ones each year. Do not kill that deer. Greet it and continue on and you will be an even greater hunter. Next you will meet a small buck. That buck will father many young ones. Do not kill it. Greet it and continue on and your power as a hunter will become greater still. At last you will meet an old buck, larger than any of the others. Its time on

Earth has been useful. Now it is ready to give itself to you. Go close to that deer and shoot it. Then greet it and thank it for giving itself to you. Do this and you will be the greatest of hunters."

The hunter did as the alligator said. He went into the forest and met the deer, killing only the old buck. He became the greatest of the hunters in his village. He told this story to his people. Many of them understood the alligator's wisdom and hunted in that way. That is why the Choctaws became great hunters of the deer. As long as they remembered to follow the alligator's teachings, they were never hungry.

**Joseph Bruchac** *has authored more than fifty books for adults and children. Of part Abenaki descent, he is a scholar of Native American culture and was honored in 1999 with the Lifetime Achievement Award of the Native Writers' Circle.*

# Cleaning Redfish with Uncle

JACK B. BEDELL

The sun never shone on fishing days.
That was a law. Everything—
the sky, the water, the dock
that held us over Bayou Dularge—
matched Uncle's gray-green slickers.

The ritual was always the same,
redfish clamped to the fillet table,
Uncle looking from dock to sky
as if to feel himself in place
before staring into the fish's eye.

It's a rule, you see. Staring
keeps the fish in place
so you can slice down from pectoral to tail
and leave only spine, guts, and gills
to throw back breathing to the water.

Uncle showed me a hundred times,
but I never stared at the eye.
Instead, I watched the graceful
fall of the fish as it slid
into the oily colors under the dock.

In my mind, I slid with it,
twitched and careened to the bottom.
I wanted to put back what Uncle took
so neatly with his blade.

**Jack B. Bedell** *was born and raised on the Gulf Coast and still lives within minutes of the water. He is an associate professor of English and creative writing at Southeastern Louisiana University and the author of several collections of poetry.*

# Jewels of the Night

SuzAnne C. Cole

young girls yearning to be beautiful
we pinch off fireflies' glowing gold
adorn dirty fingers with luminescent rings
pudgy arms with bracelets of light

**SuzAnne C. Cole,** *a former college English instructor, is the author of* To Our Heart's Content: Meditations for Women Turning 50. *She's published essays, poetry, plays, and short fiction in many magazines and anthologies, including* Newsweek, *the* Houston Chronicle, *and* Animal Blessings.

# The Soul of Southern Cooking

Kathy Starr

*Much of the traditional cooking of the Gulf Coast is closely tied to the region's flora and fauna. Freshwater and saltwater fish, game birds, wild greens, and berries are among the many ingredients gathered from the water and land to produce African-American soul food. In these excerpts from her cookbook,* The Soul of Southern Cooking, *Kathy Starr describes some of her experiences harvesting, preparing, and eating food when she was growing up in Hollandale, Mississippi.*

My love of cooking started early. I was learning from my grandmama by the time I was five years old, which was in the late fifties. She had a cafe known as the Fair Deal, and it was located over on Blue Front, across the railroad track in Hollandale. Blue Front was a string of little cafes where everybody gathered on the weekend. It was the only place blacks had to go, to get rid of the blues after a week's hard work in the cotton fields. Everybody lived for Saturday night to go to Blue Front and get a whole- or a half-order of buffalo fish or a bowl of chitterlings. People didn't like catfish then like they do now. As soon as the fishermen came by with the big buffaloes, Uncle Ira would get out in the back and start cleaning them.

The every-Saturday-night meal and the prices during my time were:

Chitterlings and Hot Sauce (50 cents a bowl)
Fried Buffalo Fish (60 cents; 1/2 order, 35 cents)
Flatdogs (15 cents)
Hamburgers (25 cents)
Regular dinners ($1.35)

My grandmama, who everybody called "Miz Bob," would always start a Saturday night with one hundred pounds of chitterlings and seventy-five pounds of buffalo. Once the people started drinking, the hunger would start, and before 11:00 P.M. all of the fish and chitterlings would be sold out. They would be eating those hamburgers and flatdogs (fried bologna sandwiches), too. . . . The Seabirds (Seeburg juke boxes) would be jammin' all up and down Blue Front with Howlin' Wolf, Muddy Waters, and B. B. King. Sometimes they would be there in person over at the Day and Night Cafe. The great blues singer Sam Chatmon came to Fair Deal often. People danced, ate, drank, and partied all night long till the break of day. . . .

My grandmama served dinner in the middle of the day. She considered it a disaster if dinner wasn't ready by twelve noon. A lot of her regular customers were farm and oil mill workers. The section workers on the Y & M V Railroad (Yazoo and Mississippi Valley, later Illinois Central) were her regular boarders. They paid her every two weeks when the railroad paid off. The girls at the pressing shop were also regulars.

Every morning about 5:00 A.M. my grandmother would get ready to put the dinners on. I remember crossing the railroad tracks on cold November mornings. The wind would be howling, and the pecans were rattling down on the tin roofs of the shotgun houses. Sometimes you could hear the towboat whistling out on the Mississippi River fourteen miles away.

We'd pass the cottonseed oil mill. Whenever it was running, it always smelled like they were making ham sandwiches or cooking fried chicken. The compress was running too, day and night, pressing those bales of cotton. When I'd get over to Fair Deal, I'd crawl up on top of the drink box under the counter and go to sleep to the steady thumping and hissing of the compress. And I'd nap until the good smells and sounds woke me up—big pots of greens and vegetable soup simmering on the stove and Grandma stirring up the corn bread. . . .

## Winter

I like to start the new year off the way I always have, the way all the black families I know do: by eating black-eyed peas and hog jowl. . . . My grandmama believes if you can have your black-eyed peas and hog jowl ready by twelve noon, you'll have a lucky year.

Back in the old days, as soon as Christmas was over and the black folks had settled up with the plantation owner, everyone started thinking about the new year. Some had made a little money, some had broken even, and some had ended up in debt. But always there was hope for the new year coming up. So New Year's Day was celebrated with family and friends.

They'd kill a hog between Christmas and New Year's if the weather was cold enough. Sometimes the men went hunting, but always the women in the family were preparing for the New Year's dinner. This is the menu Aunt Frances and my grandmama always served on New Year's Day, and I still use this menu for my New Year's dinner. It is a different meal from the great Christmas feast, but it is still wonderful and everyone looks forward to it.

*New Year's Day Dinner*
Black-eyed Peas, with Hog Jowl and Ham Stribblings
Hen/Dressing
Chitterlings
Collard Greens with Salt Meat
Candied Yams
Cranberry Sauce
Corn Bread
Dessert
Lemon Glazed Cake
Pecan Pie

## Spring

Spring in the Delta is a beautiful time. In March farmers can get in the fields and start breaking up the land and plowing. They still use the old saying that when the pecan trees bud, you can plant corn, and when the pecan buds are as big as a squirrel's ear, you can plant cotton.

When I was a child, I used to love to go out in the fields and pastures, looking for wild greens and poke sallet, and sometimes wild onions and garlic. The onions and garlic were so strong, we didn't use them often. For Easter, we always had a nice ham, and we always had mustard greens.

*Easter Dinner*
Baked Ham
Potato Salad
Mustard Greens
Candied Sweet Potatoes
Yeast Rolls

Corn Bread
Coconut Cake
Pecan Pie
Iced Tea

Spring was fishing time too, and early in the morning or late in the afternoon, we'd go down to the creek bank and throw in our lines. If it was still too chilly to sit on the ground, we'd turn our bait buckets upside down and sit on them. It was nice to come home with a string of white perch and breams to change the winter diet, and sometimes a big turtle for soup.

Gardens were planted early so the vegetables would come in as soon as possible. Blackberries and dewberries would begin to ripen all along the railroad track. (When I was a kid, we always called them wild berries, just like we called all birds, like quail and doves, wild birds.) My grandmama says if you were riding the Bigleben train from Hollandale to Leland, sometimes the conductor would let you off to pick a hat full of berries, while the train was stopped at some little station. . . .

## Summer

Summer was the busy time back in the old days. There was corn to be gathered, hay to be cut, and the last chopping and weeding of the cotton before the crop was "laid by." (This meant there was nothing left to be done until the cotton bolls opened and it was ready to be picked.) There was an old saying that "if the cotton was lappin' in the middles on the Fourth of July, you will have a good crop."

We always celebrated the Fourth of July with a picnic, either down on the creek bank or in someone's back yard. We always barbecued a pig, and one time we barbecued a goat. My great-grandfather Fleming was always in charge of the Fourth of July picnic. They would always roast a suckling pig. Early in the day, he would dig a pit and get the fire going, and by afternoon he would set the pig up on the roasting pin.

***Fourth of July Picnic***

Roast Pig with Barbecue Sauce
Potato Salad
Greens and Corn Bread
Roast Ears of Corn
Cakes and Pies
Watermelon

This is our most important holiday. The Fourth of July means freedom to blacks, freedom from slavery. Despite the fact that it really is America's Independence Day, the Fourth became associated in black people's minds with "Freedom Day." . . .

This was also the time for preserving and canning. All the

vegetables were coming in—tomatoes, okra, squash, cucumbers, peppers, watermelons, and green and red peppers. Soup mixtures were "put up," along with dill and sweet pickles, relishes and chow-chow. Plums, peaches, pears, and figs were ripe. . . .

## Fall

This is the most important time of the year—the time the farmers are getting the crop out (harvesting the cotton). It used to be that everybody was picking cotton—men, women, and children going up and down the cotton rows, dragging the long sacks from sunup to sundown. Wagons went back and forth to the gin and the oil mill. The pickers brought their lunches, a bucket of water, and quilts to put down for the babies under a nearby tree. Sometimes there was a leader (called an Eagle Rocker) who'd lean on the back of his hoe and start a song, and the others would answer. This made the long day go faster. Picking went on from late summer into fall. This was the money crop, and it was important to get all the cotton out before the heavy rains and the bad weather set in.

Pecans were beginning to fall. Persimmons were turning yellow. The older folks remember purple possum grapes and bronzy muscadines hanging from the tops of the tall trees. It was time to dig the sweet potatoes and put them in the sweet potato pump. The little shed next to the corn crib would be full of baskets of Irish potatoes, sprinkled over with lime to preserve them, black-eyed peas, crowder (field) peas, green tomatoes, onions, strings of red peppers, pumpkins, and cushaws.

Thanksgiving came in the middle of cotton-picking time,

but everyone would enjoy a nice turkey or goose, and sometimes, like in the Depression, they would be glad to have a juicy fat hen. After Thanksgiving, everyone was working on winding up the crop and waiting for settlement day. Around Christmas I can remember the farmers who were regulars at the Fair Deal Cafe would be excited about their bonuses–lump sums of money from the crop. We were excited too, since this meant more money for the cafe. Women and children were busy cooking and baking, cracking and picking out pecans and walnuts, getting ready for Christmas. This was the most joyous holiday of the year. It was time for family members to come home on visits and old friends and neighbors to take Christmas together.

Here is my grandmama's and my Christmas dinner menu. The holiday table is never considered complete if you can't fill up at least one separate table with food. She used to start cooking five or six days before Christmas, starting with her cakes, and she would cook steady coming up to Christmas.

*Christmas Dinner Main Course*

Baked Turkey
Baked Duck
Baked Ham
Duck Dressing with Giblet Gravy
Potato Salad
Cranberry Sauce
Chow-Chow
Mustard and Turnip Greens
with Salt Meat and Ham Hocks
Corn Bread
Yeast Rolls

Dessert
Coconut Cake
Jelly Cake
Caramel Cake
Pecan Pies
Sweet Potato Pies
Ambrosia
Fruit Cake

***Beverages***
Egg Nog
Iced Tea
Beer/Wine
Soda

*Formerly a nurse,* **Kathy Starr** *now runs her own catering business in Hollandale, Mississippi.*

# My Mother Returns to Calaboz

*El Calaboz, Texas*

MARGO TAMEZ

The fragmented jawbones
and comblike teeth of seagulls
sometimes wash up from the Gulf
to the levee of the river
and gather striated along the berms
where my grandfather irrigated sugarcane.

My mother, returned after forty years away,
walks there often,
hassled by INS* agents
when she goes jogging by the river.
They think she runs away from them,
that she is an illegal,
trespassing from Mexico.
Used to the invasion
she asks them how they assume,
how *exactly* do they know
if she came from here, or there?
*I am an indigenous woman,*
*born in El Calaboz, you understand?,*
she says to them in Spanish,
and they tear out,

anger spitting up with the sandy soil
behind their truck's wheels.

When I was a girl walking on the levee
with my grandfather, I thought I saw gull teeth
chopping at the soil wall.
The air was dank steam,
the scent of sand, roots,
and something living beneath the soil
deeper and older than memory.
When I put my hand beneath
the cloudy water's surface
it became a fluid form,
soft, something becoming,
something ancient.

Now the air is still heavy with heat and damp,
but smells like diesel and herbicides.
A scent reminds me of failed gestations.
My reproduction, the plants' and the water's
each struggling in the same web of survival.

When I was a girl, my grandfather taught me
to put a small clump of soil in my mouth,
and to swallow it. I watched him.
Then I did.
I used to watch the gliding and swerves
of uprooted reeds in the river's unhurried flow
to the Gulf.
I reached with all my body,

stomach on the bank of the levee,
hands and arms stretched out like an acrobat
to touch and grab their slender stems.
Once, my feet pressed into the soupy bog,
and stepping up was the sound of gurgles,
like seaweed breathing.

Now, I think I'd like to be running with mother
when she tells off the *migra,*†
listen to the bubbling duet of water and plant life
listen to their sound,
closely.
Again and again.

*Immigration and Naturalization Service
†INS agents

**Margo Tamez** *grew up in South Texas and is from a community of Spanish land grant and native peoples called El Calaboz. She now lives and works on an organic farm in southern Arizona with her husband and children. Her work has appeared in journals and anthologies, including* American Poetry Review *and* The Americas Review. *This poem will appear in* Naked Wanting, *a collection of her poetry forthcoming from the University of Arizona Press in early 2003.*

# Fig Picking

## Cassandra King

*Human prejudice—against places, other people, and other living things—stems primarily from two things: ignorance and fear. In this chapter from her novel* The St. John Show, *Cassandra King introduces us to a young girl coming to terms with her own prejudices as she joins her grandmother for an afternoon of fig picking on a hot Alabama day.*

I came to regret the day I agreed to spend my fourteenth summer with Granny Sweetwater, but never so much as when she made me go with her to Bunch Mosley's yard to pick figs. Ever since I'd arrived, all she wanted me to do was work and I was tired of it. I would've played sick like when she wanted me to milk her stinking goats, except she promised I could go to the picture show Saturday afternoon if I behaved.

Even at that I had to think about it. Granny was smart, give her that. When we went to the clinic last week for her medicine, I saw the new *Gidget* movie advertised on the marquee of The Strand and started begging then. "We'll see," was all she'd say. "Let's wait and see how you behave, whether you keep on being so sassy." So I'd been on my best behavior, not fussing and whining when she drug me with her to the pea patch or peach trees or blackberry bushes, lugging buckets. After the picking, we'd sit on the porch and shell, shuck, peel, chop, whatever, then stew, preserve, or can the stuff in her hot little kitchen. But figs! I didn't even know what they looked like.

"I dreamt about a fig tree last night," Granny told me as we walked the road to Bunch's house. I hated the road; it was paved with oyster shells and hurt my feet, even through my tennis shoes. A big shell flipped up and struck my ankle, and I hollered. It stunk out here, too. Granny lived on the river road next to the paper mill and I had to get used to the awful stench.

"I ain't even looked in Bunch's yard to see if the figs are ripe yet," she continued, not noticing I wasn't paying no attention to her. "When I dream of a fig tree, I know without looking."

I rolled my eyes. It embarrassed me the way Granny played like she was some kind of medicine woman or something, just because she was part Cherokee Indian. She wore a long bright-colored dress and cowboy hat with a silver band, and her trademark was the pipe she smoked, packed with tobacco she raised. From under the hat a long black braid without a trace of gray hung down her back. Her dark eyes were stern and unsmiling, making her look kind of mean.

It was about a mile to Bunch Mosley's house, and the sun overhead was so hot I felt like I was about to faint. Sweat poured in my eyes, and I squinted. Most of the time we picked in the early morning or late afternoon, after it'd cooled down some. But today Granny'd got it in her head she wanted to have figs for supper, so we set out right after lunch. I was afraid she'd have a sunstroke in this heat. Granny was old as dirt; she claimed she didn't know but I bet she was almost eighty.

We turned off the oyster-paved road to the dirt path that came up behind Bunch's neat white frame house, a better looking place than Granny's tin-roofed shack. At first I couldn't believe that a colored family had a better house than my own grandmother, but since Bunch was the housekeeper for the St. John family, the house was provided. Granny was always going to Bunch's, trying to make me go, too, but I wouldn't. I told her Daddy'd beat the living daylights out of me if I went into a colored person's house. Granny'd hooted and said she was glad Mama hadn't lived to see what a drunken fool Daddy'd become. The two of them had never gotten along. Daddy claimed Granny Sweetwater hated him because he and Mama eloped when she was only sixteen years old.

Granny untied the white-washed gate that led into Bunch's backyard. She held it open for me and I hesitated before going in. It was overgrown and snakey-looking, full of bushes and trees and flowers I'd never seen before. I lugged my bucket through the ankle-high grass as I followed after her. "Looks like Miss Bunch'd make Calvin get his lazy butt out here and cut the grass."

"Calvin's her baby so she spoilt him rotten," Granny chuckled, then suddenly stopped by the honeysuckle-covered fence. I almost ran into her. "Yep, they're ripe, all right," she said.

She put her hand up to shade her eyes as she looked at two big trees by the fence, and I knew with a sinking heart that these were the fig trees and they were sure ripe. Brown globes of fruit covered the skinny twisted limbs, weighing down the lower ones so that they touched the scrubby Bermuda grass beneath them.

I forgot my efforts to be good and threw my bucket down. "Don't tell me we've got to pick all of them," I cried, wiping the sweat off my face with the back of my hand.

"Now, Fern," Granny said, reaching for a fig branch and

bending it toward her, "don't you think of it that way. Think about how good them fig preserves are gonna be on our biscuits."

"I never had a preserved fig," I snorted, wrinkling my nose, "and I don't intend to start now."

Granny started plucking the figs nearest the ground, throwing them into her bucket where they made soft thudding sounds. "You don't know what's good," was all she said until I kept standing there with my hands on my hips, scowling at her. Then she got mad. "I could walk to town on those lips of yours. Get to picking or I'll wear you out, Miss Priss," she snapped at me.

I sighed loud as I could, then reached for a fat round fig hanging from the branch nearest me. "What is this thing?" I yelped when I pulled it from the stem. The fig I held in my hand looked like a woman's veined breast, leaking some kind of white milky substance. I saw that the pale green leaves were also weird, big and soft and hairy. They gave me the creeps and I stepped back in disgust. I was surprised to see Granny plop a fat brown fig in her mouth, biting it off at the stem and chewing happily. She held another one in her big old hand, as brown and spotted as the fig. "Try one," she said.

The fig was too ripe and the skin had busted to reveal a fleshy-looking pink inside. The overripe ones had fallen on the ground like dead things. Wasps and yellow jackets swarmed around them, and I shuddered. "How can you eat those nasty things, Granny?"

"Wait till you smell them cooking, you'll see," she chuckled. "Not many things on this earth smell that good. Now, hush up or no picture show for you!"

I turned and began grabbing the disgusting things, throwing them in the bucket, trying to touch their soft flesh as little as possible. Nothing to do but fill the buckets and keep my mouth shut. I knew Granny well enough to know she meant what she said.

At least the figs were easy to pick and I used both hands, not looking Granny's way as I flung them in the bucket. "Bucket's full," I was able to tell her finally, straightening up. Seemed like hours but probably hadn't taken half a one. The tree was so full I'd not even had to move, me picking one tree and Granny the other. But when I turned to her tree, Granny was gone.

"Granny? Where—" Before I could get the words out, I saw that she'd gone to Bunch's back porch and was now coming back, carrying an empty fertilizer bucket. Turning my head, I spotted her own bucket, propped against the tree trunk, full.

"I hope you're not bringing that bucket to put more figs in," I cried. I was so sweaty my eyes were stinging and watering. Granny'd tried to get me to wear a hat but I'd refused. In spite of my dark complexion, I'd already burned and peeled a couple of times this summer. Now the top of my head felt like it was on fire, and my arms were red and hot. Granny'd tried to make me wear one of her dresses instead of my shorts and sleeveless shirt, but I wouldn't be caught dead in one of her tacky old dresses.

"Them figs is for us," Granny said, nodding her head toward our buckets. "Now we're gonna pick Bunch some." And she made her way up to the tree, grabbing a branch right above her head. "We about picked this one clean. Shimmy up your tree, girl. We'll have to get to the top to pick another mess."

I looked at the gnarled trees and shook my head. My tree was about a foot taller than Granny's but the trunk wasn't much bigger than my arm. "Shoot, Granny," I protested. "That tree ain't big enough to climb. It'll break."

"Huh! Light as you are, you couldn't break a peach tree. Get your fanny-butt up far enough to reach those top branches." I sighed loud but grabbed a limb over my head and hopped up, pulling upright and positioning myself between two small branches at the top of the tree. I wanted nothing more than to pick those stupid figs and get it over with.

I bent a heavy-laden branch over so she could reach it and, with a frown, she picked it clean, her brown hands moving like the wind. Then I moved to reach another branch, higher up.

"I hate this stupid tree, Granny," I cried when the soft fuzzy leaves brushed my skin like human hands. "It looks like it's alive." The leaves, like the figs, leaked a milklike substance when broken. I shuddered, averting my eyes.

"All trees is alive," Granny said, shading her eyes with her hands as she watched me pull a branch toward her.

"I mean, like a person. Like something—real!" I said.

"This tree is real, Fern," Granny said, squinting as she stripped the branch of its fruit. "It has feelings just like me or you. It's proud of itself for giving so many figs today. Your fussing'll make it feel bad."

"Oh, sure," I laughed. "I believe being out in the sun has made your brain soft."

Before I realized what was happening, Granny grabbed my arm, jerking me down from my perch. I reached for a low-hanging branch frantically as she pulled me down beside her. I fell on my feet but she jerked me up.

"I don't know where you got that smart mouth of yours, Fern Cooper," she growled at me, giving me a shake, "but it weren't from your mama!"

I glared back at her, trying to think of something to say. Her big rough hand on my arm was hurting because of the sunburn, but I wasn't about to say so, giving her the satisfaction of telling me I should've covered myself like she said.

"I bet you made Mama pick these stupid old figs when she was my age and that's how come she ran off and married Daddy, to get away from you," I cried, my eyes suddenly smarting with tears.

Tightening her grip on my arm, Granny reached to break off a switch as I tried to pull away from her. Looking over her shoulder, I saw Bunch Mosley coming through the tall grass toward us. An enormously fat colored woman, she was dressed in a black uniform of a silky material, except for the white apron, which stuck out from her big body like one of those skirts ballerinas wear. I had an idea that she'd been watching us fuss from the porch and showed herself at a critical moment.

"Here comes Bunch Mosley," I hissed at Granny, and she dropped my arm.

"Well, Lord-a-mercy me," Bunch said, laughing her loud laugh, throwing her head back. I'd never seen her without bright red lipstick on, her mouth so wide it was like a pink cave splitting her face in two, showing the wide gap between her front teeth. "Look who done come picked my figs! I can near about taste them preserves of yours, Posey Sweetwater."

"I dreamt of a fig tree last night," Granny told her, thankfully forgetting me and my sassiness. "So I knowed it was time to make preserves for supper."

I relaxed, rubbing my arm and taking a deep breath. I knew I'd barely escaped getting a whipping. Granny'd never hit me, but I'd seen her switch my brothers good for sassing her.

Bunch bent and looked at the full buckets as she smacked her lips. "I want you to look at all them figs!" she declared. There was something different about her, and I blinked in surprise. Today was the first time I'd ever seen her without her hair tied up, a scarf turbaned around it. I was astonished that her kinky salt-and-pepper hair was as short as a man's. It made her look funny and I giggled. Big and fat with so little hair, she looked like the plump brown figs with the small stems on top.

"Posey Sweetwater, get on and get them figs going," Bunch laughed again, rolling her eyes at Granny. "Then fo' dark, I'm gonna come sit on your porch just to smell them cooking!"

Granny shook her head. "No'm. I'm gonna pick you a mess before they get too ripe. I'm fixing to get Fern to shimmy back up the tree—"

"Uh-uh, you ain't doin' no such thing," Bunch interrupted. "I told Calvin to pick them figs and I'd pay him. He be mad if y'all get 'em first."

Granny looked at Bunch skeptically, narrowing her eyes, but Bunch ignored her, turning to me and smiling. "Besides, I need Miss Fern to help me do somethin', if you'll let her."

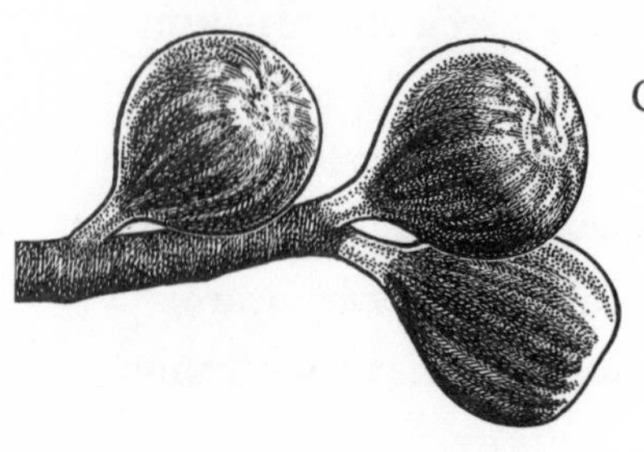

I drew my breath in. "Oh, *please,* Granny—"

"Huh! Reckon I might be too soft in the noggin to decide whether you can or not," she grunted, but there was a twinkle in her dark eyes.

I wanted to hug her neck, hot and sweaty as we both were, but Granny wasn't affectionate. She'd not hugged me since I'd been here. "Granny, I'm sorry I sassed you. Please—"

"Aw, you ain't helping no how," she sighed. "Go on with Bunch and behave yourself."

Bunch shook her head as she stood watching us, hands on her hips. "You forgot what it's like to be a young girl and have to work in the sun, Posey. 'Sides, I'm gonna trade you this girl for Calvin. I'll send his sorry black fanny out to carry them figs home."

I was so glad to get away from Granny and the figs that I practically ran after Bunch Mosley as she started back toward her house. Only after I stumbled up the back porch steps I realized I'd actually be entering a colored person's house, something I never thought I'd do.

We went into the kitchen, and I looked around me in amazement. It was as fine as any white person's house I'd ever been in. Bunch's kitchen was painted butter yellow and had starched white curtains in the windows. Both windows had fans in them, going full blast, making it much cooler than Granny's. It was so clean that the appliances and the stovetop gleamed like new. I couldn't help but feel even more ashamed that Granny's house—and my own, too, for that matter—was so much worse than a colored family's.

I could see part of their living room, drapes pulled tight against the hot sun, with a small television, gray-and-white images flickering in the semidarkness. Neither Granny nor my family had a television set yet. I'd only watched the programs a couple of times, at my teacher's house. "Calvin Mosley, turn that thing off and go help Miz Posey Sweetwater carry two buckets of figs to her house," Bunch hollered.

"Yes'm, but I sho' ain't going in!" Calvin yelled back, and I giggled.

Bunch turned to me, rolled her eyes, then nodded her small round head toward a hallway leading off the kitchen. "Come on, sugar-baby. You gonna help me make yo' Granny a batch of yeast rolls for y'all's supper, but let's get you cleaned up before you blister any worse. You a sight if I ever seen one!"

I couldn't believe the green-tiled bathroom she led me to. It was twice as big as Granny's and she had it fixed up real nice, with a green crocheted thing on the commode and a ruffled skirt under the sink, matching the flowered curtains at the window. Even the tub was green.

"You've fixed your house up real pretty, Miss Bunch," I told her, breathing deeply of the sweet talcum powder, a scent that I'd first smelled on her.

She seemed pleased as she nodded toward the sink. "There's you a washrag and some soap. Let's see if we can git you looking better."

I couldn't believe my eyes when I looked in the medicine-cabinet mirror, and I turned to Bunch, horrified. "Oh, Lord, Miss Bunch—look at me!" My hair was matted and tangled, wet with sweat and sticking to my head. My face was not only blood-red but filthy, my nose peeling in strips. My arms were covered with welts from insect bites and tree scratches. The white milky stuff from the figs made me feel sticky all over.

"You a mess, that's for sho'. Get yourself washed up, then come across the hall to my room," Bunch said, going out and closing the door after her.

After washing myself gingerly, wincing as the soap stung my burnt skin, I left the green bathroom and peeked in the bedroom across the hall. It was big and sunny, with flowery wallpaper and heavy brown-painted furniture. Standing by a mirrored dresser, Bunch motioned for me to sit down on the cushioned bench there. "Least you clean. Now let's see what we can do with that mess of hair."

I was too surprised to yell when Bunch grabbed my hair and started brushing the tangles out, hard. Our eyes met in the mirror and she threw her head back and laughed, her brown eyes bright. "Now don't you worry none, baby. This here brush ain't never been used. No colored hairs in it."

My face flamed red, making the sunburn even brighter. Bunch nodded toward a blue Vick's Salve jar on the dresser. "Rub some of that stuff on your face."

I opened the jar and stuck my fingers in, then looked up at her, shuddering in disgust. "It looks like snot, Miss Bunch."

"Your Granny fixed it for me, so no telling what it be. Might be gator boogers." She threw back her head and laughed at the expression on my face. "Old Bunch be teasing you, baby. Ain't nothin' but aloe juice, but it'll make your face quit burning."

I patted the green slimy stuff on as Bunch began pulling even harder on my hair with the brush, jerking my head back. When I realized she was plaiting my hair I swallowed and squirmed nervously, not daring to meet her eyes. I hoped I didn't turn out looking like a pickaninny. When she finished, I was surprised. Instead of cornrows she'd made a tightly braided plait that encircled my head like a wreath, high off my neck, and cool. She leaned over and gave me a sweet-smelling hug when she saw my smile in the mirror. "I had me a baby girl once, but she didn't live no time, hardly. She would have been about your age now."

I didn't know what to say to that. I looked up and saw her watching me. "Did you know my Mama, Miss Bunch?"

She nodded. "Sho' did. You the spitting image of her. I know it hurts Posey to see how much you look like her. I thought she was gon' grieve herself to death when that girl died! She's been so happy you finally come to stay with her she can hardly stand it."

"She don't act like it. She's mean to me and makes me work all the time," I sniffed.

Bunch chuckled. "Don't you pay no mind to Posey's talk. She do that to hide how happy she is that you here. After all these years your daddy let you come, and now she's scared it's been too long, that you won't come back. Come on now, baby. Let's go fix them rolls."

I spent the rest of the afternoon with Bunch in her bright yellow kitchen, helping her mix up yeast rolls and roll them out, folding them into pocketbook shapes and brushing them with melted butter. I was actually enjoying myself, though we didn't do anything but work, just like at Granny's. But Bunch was jolly and fun and didn't fuss like Granny did when I made a mess. I didn't sass her like I did Granny, either. I almost hated to see the sun going down. Bunch'd already told me we wouldn't cook the rolls; we'd take them all risen and ready to pop in the oven so they'd be fresh baked for our supper tonight.

Me and Bunch didn't talk as we walked the oyster-shell road to Granny's house, each with a pan of rolls in hand, the pans covered with a dishcloth, bleached white and soft as a baby diaper. The rolls gave off a rich yeasty smell, and as we climbed the cement blocks leading up to the front porch of Granny's house, I realized I was starving. Something else was in the air besides the yeasty aroma of the rolls. The awful river smell had been replaced by the most heavenly fragrance I've ever breathed, like all the spices of the world had been thrown together to simmer over a fire of burning flowers. I turned to Bunch wide-eyed as she waddled up the steps behind me, turning her hips sideways to navigate the narrow blocks. "What on earth is that smell?" I asked her.

Bunch laughed. "Baby, that's them figs your Granny's cooking. You just in time for supper."

We went through the cluttered living room into the steaming little kitchen. Sure enough, Granny was stooped over the tiny stove, stirring a big washpan full of syrupy caramel-brown figs, looking and smelling completely different than they did on the tree.

Granny nodded approval when we came in. "They done," she announced solemnly. She held out a lard bucket toward Bunch. "I got y'all some preserves cooled off to tote back, Bunch."

Bunch put her pan of rolls down on the cabinet. "Much obliged, Posey. And we made you some yeast rolls," she told her. "They ready to go straight in the oven."

Granny nodded her head toward the stove. "It's on. I was about to make some biscuits, but I'd ruther have them rolls. Stick 'em in the oven, girl, and give Bunch her dishrags back."

I did as she told me, jerking my head back at the heat from the oven. "Did y'all have a big time this afternoon?" Granny asked me. She was still dressed in her long dress, and sweat covered her shiny broad face, dripping from her chin. With the rolls cooking in the oven, it was so hot in the cramped little kitchen that it was hard to breathe.

"Yes'm, we sure did," I nodded. "Miss Bunch has the nicest house, and she showed me how to make rolls. When we eat all these, I'll make us some more."

"I gotta git on back now, git our supper," Bunch smiled, moving toward the door with her lard bucket of fig preserves.

"You welcome to stay and eat with us," Granny told her, but Bunch was shaking her head before she could finish. "I hope you didn't let this girl pester you too much this afternoon," Granny added, cutting her dark eyes toward me.

"Lord-a-mercy, no. We had us a big time," Bunch said.

Granny poked me in the ribs with her elbow. "What you say to Miz Bunch, Fern Cooper?"

I turned toward her and smiled. "I appreciate it, Miss Bunch. I want you to show me how to do my hair like this sometime."

Bunch reached back in to hug me before she went out the door.

The kitchen was so little the three of us could barely stand in there together. It was a little better after Bunch left, but still unbearably hot.

"We can't eat in the house tonight, Granny," I groaned. "Let's take our plates out on the front porch and eat our supper."

Granny looked at me slyly. "Reckon you'll have to fry you some eggs since you don't want to eat no figs."

I shrugged as I grabbed the big wooden spoon sticking up from the cooked figs and stirred them slowly. "I might eat a few."

Granny chuckled and shook her head. "You're about the stubbornest girl I ever saw in my life," she said.

"Reckon I take after my granny, then." I raised a spoonful

of thick caramel figs to my mouth and blew on them before touching my tongue to the edge. It was so good I ate the whole thing, burning my mouth. Then I licked the spoon.

"You wash that before putting it back in those preserves," Granny snapped. "And I smell them rolls. Git them out before they burn, you hear me?"

I ate so much supper I like to have made myself sick. I left Granny sitting on the porch in her rocking chair and went to bed, so full I was miserable. Before I went in, I stopped by the rocker and put my hand on her big brown arm hesitantly, then quickly removed it.

"Goodnight, Granny Sweetwater. I'm going on to bed now," I said to her. It was hot and airless, but thunder was rumbling in the distance, so maybe it would rain.

"Goodnight, Mary Fern," I thought Granny said. She was smoking her pipe and she didn't take it out of her mouth.

"That was Mama," I told her, "not me. I'm just plain Fern." I didn't think she heard me because she didn't move, not even to rock. I shrugged and went inside.

When I went to bed I lay on the cot by the window and listened to the night sounds, the frogs from the river and the crickets and mosquitoes. I heard the thunder again, and then I heard the sound I'd been listening for: Granny's rocker, creaking as she rocked and smoked her pipe, looking out over the black starless night. The sweet-smelling pipe smoke floated like angel wings through the front window and hung over my head.

In spite of the heat, I fell off to sleep. Like Granny, I dreamed of fig trees, but my dream-trees were shaped like people, with twisted limbs that reached out deformed arms to me. I saw bent tree-people standing in a circle, except their feet were roots, buried in the ground. I walked among them and they touched my braided hair with soft green leaf-hands. Then I saw why they stood in a circle. In the center was an old fig tree, bent and brown and gnarled with age. Underneath it was Granny Sweetwater, laid out in death, her big brown arms folded over her chest. The tree dropped figs all over her body, so ripe they fell like tears.

*A native of the Wiregrass area of Lower Alabama,* **Cassandra King** *currently resides in the South Carolina low country. She has written three novels, including* Making Waves in Zion, The Sunday Wife, *and a novel-in-progress,* The St. John Show, *from which this excerpt is taken.*

# Public School

## Abe Louise Young

Half the students come to class
in high, black rubber boots.
They leave for work before the bell
to haul in from the shrimp boats.

The science teacher repeats
over and over that matter can never
be created or destroyed:
it only changes form.

He underlines the words with colored chalk
as if they are a proven consolation.
In her tin trailer across
from the refinery, the math teacher

remainders compost:
solitude, kitchen scrap,
onions, okra, carrot tops.
Her slowly growing heap of questions,

high as a fire hydrant.
How do we measure the value of our labors?

This is a neighborhood
of sofas on porches,

stunted orchards, integration,
hunters, and washed hands.
Leaning against
the chalkboard after class

leaves sweat prints
of the science teacher's torso.
He confides in the math teacher
that he privately believes

in evolution—but that he's sure
all people are divine.

*A Louisiana native,* **Abe Louise Young** *is currently exploring low-impact living on the coastline of California. She is a teacher, writer, and three-time recipient of the Academy of American Poet's Anne Bradstreet Prize.*

Wild Lives

# Crows in the Yard

KATRINKA MOORE

Crows swooped into trees in the yard
Landing and cawing cawing
Bouncing on high thin branches
Cawing and flapping flapping

Flapping their wings and landing
Cawing and bouncing cawing
Diving at squirrels on the tree trunks
Cawing and flapping flapping

Swooping and flying swooping
Flapping and up, flying beyond
Beyond the trees in the yard

Flying and cawing cawing
Cawing and flying
Flying

**Katrinka Moore** *grew up near Friendswood, Texas, then moved to New York to work as a dancer and choreographer. She currently teaches writing at Long Island University in Brooklyn and has published her poetry in such magazines as the* Little Magazine, Brooklyn Review, *and* Earth's Daughters.

# Mosquito Blues

DOROTHY SHAWHAN

*Given all the incredible creatures that preen and burrow and prowl along the Gulf Coast, it's unfortunate—but probably inevitable—that the one that gets the most attention is a tiny, two-winged whiner.*

Hawaii has tarantulas, Texas has rattlers, Florida alligators, Minnesota black flies, and even Eden had a snake. You're whistling Dixie if you don't admit that in the Delta we have our own special reason to sing the blues–the mosquito.

In almost any Delta scene mosquitoes play a key role. I've seen them change a genteel garden party into a leg-slapping, foot-stomping, arm-waving blood bath; I've heard a single mosquito buzz sleeping households into hysterics in the middle of the night; I've watched neighbors virtually disappear from the community because a mosquito swarm took up right outside the kitchen door.

Ask any Deltan the disadvantages in living here, and chances are a hundred to one that a mosquito will turn up somewhere in the answer. But if you're planning to move to get away from them, good luck. The only place on planet Earth from which mosquitoes haven't been reported is the Antarctic (and that could be because there's nobody there to report). Even the North Pole has a mosquito problem. Not surprising when you consider the 2,600 species loose in the world, all of which I believe are represented in the Delta, or might as well be.

Old-timers say mosquitoes weren't always this bad around the Delta. The rice, they say, the rice fields are bringing them in like flies. Suggest that to a farmer, though, and they'll act like you've attacked Mom, apple pie, and Chevrolet. That's running water in those rice fields, they say, and mosquitoes won't breed in fresh running water.

Well, I don't know, but mosquitoes aren't famous for being choosy about their breeding places. Many species can breed in fresh or salt water (some need only seven days from egg to adult). In Trinidad they breed in bromeliads. They've been found flourishing in steamy hot alkaline pools around a volcano in Uganda and in tanks of hydrochloric acid in India. Compared to those, a Delta rice field must be paradise.

Mosquitoes will bite almost anything that moves—not just people but dogs, cattle, birds, even reptiles. But only the female bites; she needs the blood to mature her eggs and make more mosquitoes. Despite their bloodthirsty reputations, mosquitoes are allegedly vegetarians who feed on nectar and plant juices, though I've never seen them do it.

If you're a person mosquitoes love to bite, you may or may not want to know it's because of your body odor. Somehow the way you smell turns them on. Experts say mosquitoes will have as hosts only those who smell right.

While most of what mosquitoes dispense in the Delta is aggravation, time was when they wiped out whole populations of towns, devastated herds, and brought economic ruin. Throughout history mosquitoes have been at the center of medical, social, political, and economic issues all over the world. They spread such plagues as yellow fever, encephalitis, malaria, and heartworms in dogs. Obviously, with a record like that, there ought to be a law against them. As it turns out, there is.

Mosquitoes have been against the law in this country for years. Mississippi's mosquito abatement laws go back to 1928, but our mosquitoes haven't got the word yet. For those who want to keep up with the latest in legislation, the American Mosquito Control Association puts out an official publication called *Mosquito News.*

Seems we've tried almost every kind of control—getting rid of the breeding places, invoking the help of the dragonfly, mosquito fish, and purple martin; even releasing genetically incompatible males. In Cleveland we have the mosquito truck, which comes trailing streams of insecticide about six each summer evening. I'm sure the mosquito truck means well, but I soon learned, after near asphyxiation, not to have the attic fan on when it passed by.

The award for the best title of a mosquito publication goes to an Oakland, California, public information pamphlet entitled *Mosquitoes Are Unnecessary* (kind of like evil). One of this pamphlet's hottest tips is that goldfish eat mosquito eggs and larvae and so are good to have around, but that goldfish will *not* leap in the air and take a mosquito on the wing. Undoubtedly.

Despite their being illegal, mosquitoes continue to bite, and worse yet, to buzz. If you're like me, you'd rather be bitten than buzzed. I wouldn't mind being bitten so much if mosquitoes could just do it quietly. I can snooze through a bite, but not that terrible hum that signals the end of a good night's sleep.

It may comfort you to know that both males and females hum, so everything that buzzes may not bite. The sound is made by high wing-beat frequency. The female's humming is slightly lower than the male's; she uses it to attract him.

According to a West African folktale, that whole buzzing business began years ago when a mosquito bored an iguana half crazy with a tale about a farmer digging sweet potatoes that were as big as she (the mosquito) was. The iguana said he didn't have to listen to that nonsense, stuck a stick in each ear, and crawled off through the reeds.

Consequently the iguana didn't hear the python speak to him, the python took offense, decided there was a plot, and set off a chain of events that infected all of the creatures in the jungle with a bad case of paranoia.

Finally, jungle life reached such a state of discord that the King of the Beasts investigated and traced the trouble back to the mosquito. But the mosquito hid out and was never brought to justice. She still suffers from a guilty conscience, though, and is always whining in people's ears to ask if everyone is still angry.

You bet they are. She should know that by now.

The mosquito has become such a part of the folklore in the South that we tend to think of it as peculiarly our own institution. B. A. Botkin, in a book called *Treasury of Southern Folklore,* has recorded a number of mosquito tales.

As one might expect, Texas has produced some of the biggest mosquitoes ever. Houstonians claim that their mosquitoes wear 45-inch undershirts. In Galveston, town fathers include mosquitoes in the cow ordinance, while other Texans say the truth is that mosquitoes on the Texas coast are rarely bigger than an ordinary mockingbird.

Mississippi's mosquitoes are no slouches either. Ruth Bass of Hazlehurst put together some lore about them back in 1938. In one story an unfortunate traveler through the state hitched his horse by the side of a creek to go look for a ford, and when he came back the mosquitoes had "et up his horse, chawed up his saddle, and was a-pitchin' that horse's shoes to see who'd get the bridle."

An even worse predicament was that of Mississippian Bill Jenkins, who woke up one night to find himself being carried through the air by two mosquitoes. One asked the other if they should eat Bill there or hide him in the swamp for later. The other mosquito replied, "I speck we better eat him here. If we take him down to that swamp some of them big skeeters is liable to take him away from us."

From Louisiana comes this proverb in Creole dialect: *Maringouin perdi so temps quand li pique caiman.* (The mosquito loses his time when he tries to sting the alligator.)

Buzz off, in other words.

One popular belief in Southern folklore is that holding your breath while a mosquito bites you makes her unable to withdraw her bill. Then you can swat her good. Personally, I'd rather swat *before* she starts to bite.

Another favorite idea is that mosquitoes don't bite during an eclipse. My brother-in-law stood out in a mosquito swarm at two A.M. during the last eclipse and claimed they didn't bite him. They never do, though. Body odor.

Tall tales about the mosquito are not confined to historical folklore; they're being created daily all around us. For example, I have a student who claims his aunt died of mosquito inhalation in her own front yard last summer. . . .

**Dorothy Shawhan** *was born in Tupelo, Mississippi, and grew up in Verona. She is now a professor of English at Delta State University.*

# Why Alligator Hates Dog

*A Cajun Story*

J. J. Reneaux

*When J. J. Reneaux was a young girl, a flood washed a large alligator up into her neighborhood in southern Louisiana. She noticed that although the alligator ignored the shouts and shrieks of children, it hissed and snapped at her barking hound dog. Some time later, a local Cajun woman told her this story, which offers an explanation for the alligator's behavior. Like other Cajun tales, this one is sprinkled with French words and phrases, including the term "M'su"—short for Monsieur, or Mister.*

M'su Cocodrie, the alligator, was once king of all the swamp and the bayous. All the critters cut a wide circle 'round ol' Cocodrie lest they wind up in his belly. Even Man with his traps and guns was wary of M'su Cocodrie. One snap of those jaws and a fella could lose an arm, a leg, or even his life. M'su Cocodrie enjoyed the respect and fear of everybody—everybody, that is, except for *les chiens,* the dogs. How those dogs loved to tease and mock him—from a safe distance, of course!

Back in those days, M'su Cocodrie lived in a deep, dark, muddy hole in the bank of the bayou, not far from the *cabane* of Man and his pesky dogs. In the evening he loved to curl up in his hole and take a little nap before he went hunting for his supper. But just as he was dozing off, the dogs up at the *cabane* would start carryin' on, howlin', whinin', barkin', teasin', till he thought he'd go mad!

They'd howl out, "M'suuuu Cocodrie! M'suuuuu Cocodrie! Come and get us if you dare." And ooowhee! Alligator couldn't even do a thing about it, 'cept gnash those big ol' sharp teeth, thump his tail, and wait for one of those dogs to get just a little too close.

"One of these days I'm gonna get them dogs," he'd hiss. "I'll teach them to mock me, the King o' the Swamp!"

Now, one day Hound Dog came running down the bank of the bayou. I mean he was hot on the trail of Lapin, the rabbit. Thumpity, thumpity, thump. But that rabbit was too smart-smart. She led that dog right up to Alligator's hole. Well, Lapin easily jumped across, but Dog fell straight down that hole and found himself snout to snout with M'su Cocodrie. Hound Dog knew he was trapped and he better do some fast talkin' if he was gonna get out of there alive.

"Arrrhoooo," howled Hound Dog. "*Comment ça va?* How's it goin'?"

"Sooooo, at last you come to pay me a visit, hmmmm?" hissed Alligator. "Every evenin' you dogs call out, 'M'suuuu Cocodrie, come and get us!' Well, now, that's exactly what I'm gonna do. I'm gonna get you, and I'm gonna grind you into mincemeat, you miserable, mangy mutt!"

"Oh, *mais non, mon ami,*" whined Dog. "But no, my friend. Surely you did not think that my friends and I would insult you, the mighty King o' the Swamp. Oh, *mais jamais! Pas du tout!* We were only callin' you to join us for supper. We did not call out, 'Come and get us'—we called out, 'Come and get it, come and get it.' You see, every evenin' our master brings us a big bowl filled with delicious scraps of meat and bones. We call for you to come and get it, to come and join us for supper. But you never come, *mon padnat.*"

"Hmmm, is that so?" asked M'su Cocodrie.

"Oh, *mais oui!* Come this very evenin' and dine with us. For you, we will save the very best," said Dog.

"Hmm," said M'su Cocodrie, "but what of your master, the man?"

"Oh, do not worry about him. Us dogs will keep watch. If we see our master comin', we'll warn you in plenty of time and you can escape. Come and join us. We will save the very best scraps for you. After all, *mon ami,* shouldn't the King o' the Swamp eat as good as us poor dogs?"

Now, M'su Cocodrie was a powerful and fearsome creature, for sure. But he wasn't overly blessed with what you call the smarts. He thought with his stomach and he acted on the advice of his mighty appetite. So he agreed to come for supper, and he let that rascal, Dog, escape the crush of his jaws.

That evening Alligator crawled up the bank of the bayou all the way to the *cabane.* When he got to the steps of the *galerie,* the porch, he stopped and looked around, for he feared the master might be somewhere about. But the dogs started whinin', "Come up, come up, M'su Cocodrie. Our master is not here. Do you see our master? Do you hear our master? It is safe, M'su Cocodrie. You can have your pick o' the scraps. Come up and get it, M'su, come and get it!"

M'su Cocodrie looked for sure. He didn't see a thing. He listened and all was quiet. So he climbed up the steps to the *galerie,* draggin' that big, heavy tail behind him. But no sooner had he tasted one bite of those juicy scraps than the dogs started carrying on, howlin', whinin', barkin', teasin', and their master came running out to see what all the ruckus was about.

When Man saw M'su Cocodrie on his porch, he took a club and started beating him on the snout, yelling for his wife to fetch his gun. And if that wasn't bad enough, those snarling dogs leaped on M'su Cocodrie and began to bite him on his tail. Poor Alligator was lucky to escape back down his hole with his life!

Well, ever since that time Alligator hates Dog. He floats in the water like a half-sunk log with only those big eyes peering out. He's waiting and watching for one of those dogs to come just a little too close. This time Dog won't be able to trick M'su Cocodrie. These days ol' Alligator is a lot smarter. He's learned his lesson. And if M'su Cocodrie were here today, why, he'd tell you himself, for true, "Believe nothin' you hear, *mon ami,* and only half of what you see, hmmmm?"

**J. J. Reneaux** *is a nationally acclaimed storyteller. She grew up in a Cajun family, surrounded by the stories, music, food, and culture of rural communities in southeastern Texas and southern Louisiana. Her material has been gathered on front porches, school playgrounds, and fishing trips, as well as at nursing homes, airports, and neighborhood dances called* fais-dodos.

# The Season of Jellyfish

STUART DYBEK

It's the season of jellyfish,
the sea crowded with lavender plasms
and vague stings. Young squid,
still translucent, patrol, luminous
against the blue water of late afternoon.
In this season night shimmers
phosphorescent with stars and diatoms. The oars
raise floating weeds like wigs of radium.
The mackerel weave trails of light.

**Stuart Dybek** *is the author of two collections of stories and a book of poems. His work appears regularly in magazines such as* Harper's, *the* New Yorker, *and* Poetry.

# Kenzie's Plunge into Paradise

BONNIE J. DOERR

*The Florida Keys are a chain of tiny islands that stretch for 126 miles off the southern tip of Florida. People who spend time in the Keys may be treated to the sight of roseate spoonbills, mangrove cuckoos, loggerhead sea turtles, and a rare mammal species found nowhere else on Earth.*

Nothing was the same here. Not even the sun.

Mornings had been kind in Kenzie's New York apartment. Sunrise was gentle. It filtered through oak and maple trees before it peeked around her window shades. Here, on Big Pine Key, Florida, a rural island at the edge of the continent, the sun had no mercy. Without warning, its brilliant shards of light attacked her through the naked windowpanes.

Was it going to be like this every morning, she wondered? What a rude introduction to a place Nana called "Paradise."

Wasn't it enough that she'd been yanked out of St. Joe's Prep, that she'd lost all her friends, her swim team, everything she'd known all twelve years of her life? And admit it, Kenzie, she said to herself, that goes for Dad, too. I drove him nuts, she thought. He just gave up and left us. Now look where I am.

The glaring sunlight jolted Kenzie back to reality. Just Mom and me, she thought, living in Nana's stilt house, starting over in the middle of nowhere. She propped her elbows on the railing, cupped her face in her hands, and stared down at the man-made canal twenty to thirty feet below.

This was her first good look at Grandpa's dock. It had been dark when they arrived last night. The dock, a narrow concrete walkway about thirty feet long, ran the width of the property. On the other side of the canal were two rickety wooden docks paired with tired little boats.

The canal, wider than a country road, was a raw, steeply walled canyon blasted out of coral rock. It came to a dead end five houses to her left.

How far was it to the ocean? Her eyes followed the canal in the other direction. All she saw was a mass of scraggly trees and overgrown bushes. No ocean, no more houses, and not a sign of life anywhere.

Like the others, Nana's house was built up on concrete pillars twelve to fifteen feet in the air. For what? Kenzie didn't get it. How could the water possibly get that high? Two of the houses were completely shuttered. Closed up like a ski resort in summer. This place is deserted, she thought. Boring. Some paradise. She wasn't sure she'd ever forgive her mom for accepting a new nursing position and bringing her here.

The absence of sound was unsettling: no voices through the walls, no horns, no sirens, not even the ding of an elevator. She focused and heard the soft hoo-hrrooo of doves and a hoarse croak as a white heron took flight. In the breeze, coconut palm fronds gently clicked, like coasting bicycle wheels.

Something splashed. Fish, she thought. The only fish she'd ever seen outside of an aquarium were behind a glass counter on ice. She went down to the end of the dock.

She heard another splash and saw ripples spreading on the

dark water. She walked the length of the dock searching for the source. What was in there?

She jumped off the concrete and climbed over rocks and roots toward the disturbance but heard no more splashes. She found an opening in the mangroves along the canal and pushed her way to the water's edge.

Way down the canal something was swimming in jerky circles, round and round, over and over. She shielded her eyes against the glare of the sun and realized what it was: a nose and eyes. It's a little dog! she thought. It can't get out.

"Mom, wake up!" she yelled toward the bedroom window. "Hey, Mom, get up! There's a dog in the canal. He's trapped." She saw the head go under.

"Mom, hurry up! He's drowning!"

I can't jump in. I'd never get out either. It's sheer rock, too steep, she thought. I need a boat.

"Help!" she screamed again. "Somebody, anybody, help!" Searching for an opening, she raced along the tangle of trees that lined the canal.

If I could find a tree limb with lots of branches, she thought, I could toss it in the water. He could get his front legs on it.

Kenzie ducked under buttonwood limbs and emerged on the very edge of the canal. The dog's nose surfaced near her and circled again. "Swim, little guy. Don't give up," she said.

Hanging over the water was a promising branch. She reached for it. Rocks rolled beneath her feet. She looked down and saw exposed roots where the bank was crumbling. Her heels slipped. Kenzie's heart leaped to her throat. She slid further. The ground collapsed. She grabbed for the branch but caught only leaves. "Aiee!" Kenzie squealed as she plunged into the canal. A landslide of gravel tumbled after her.

She hadn't expected to sink so far. Don't panic, she told herself. Relax. It's only water. She heard her coach's voice, "Kick! Kick, ladies. Kick!" She kicked and shot to the surface gasping for breath.

She spun and saw the dog. Her eyes were burning like crazy. What was going on? she thought. Was it the salt water? Or something else in the water? She winced and squeezed her eyes shut.

Swimming in saturated clothes was awkward, but her muscles responded to hours of practice. Blindly, she swam toward the dog. She had to reach it before it went under again. Between spits and sputters, she reassured it. "I'm coming, fella! I'm almost there."

She heard frantic snorting and realized she was nearly on top of the dog. With her next stroke she touched its head. Finding its long pointed ears, she slid a hand down its neck. Yes—a collar! she thought. She grabbed it.

Terrified bleating pierced the air. What kind of dog is this? she wondered. Its thrashing feet whacked her. They were hard for paws, Kenzie thought. She squinted to get a better look. But the animal seemed more frightened than before and splashed a stinging spray into her eyes.

She concentrated on staying afloat. No problem, she thought. At school, she'd always been the one to demonstrate pulling a panicked swimmer to safety. Coach should see her now.

How was she going to get out, though? There was no way she could make it all the way back to the dock. Just start swimming, she told herself. Maybe there's a bare root where the canal collapsed. She could hang on to a root until someone heard her.

Kenzie tightened her grip on the collar. With her left arm, she held the little dog as close to her chest as possible. She struggled forward, stroking with her right arm. Kick, stroke, pull. Kick, stroke, pull.

The creature was no longer fighting. Its pitiful whimpers turned into catlike mewings. "Don't die," she begged. "Please don't die."

She tried again. "Help! Help! I can't get out of the canal. Somebody, help!" Kenzie had never before regretted that her mother was such a sound sleeper.

Kick, stroke, pull. Kick, stroke, pull. The dog was now totally immobile and chillingly quiet.

With the next stroke Kenzie reached the wall. She groped among the rocks until she found a securely anchored root. Calm down, she said to herself. Breathe. Slow and deep. It's just like hanging on the side of the pool between laps. So what if I'm holding a smelly, wet dog. So what if my eyes are on fire and my arm is breaking.

She heard a sound like wood banging against metal. What was that? she thought. An oar?

She risked a peek. A splash bounced off the rocks into her face. She blinked. But through her lens of tears, she could see no farther than the strange looking dog.

The little waves kept coming and the sound grew louder. "Help, help! Over here!"

Suddenly she heard a clatter, a bump, and a male voice. "Did you think I was blind? No way I'm going to pass up this record catch. Bring the deer to the boat."

The what? she thought. Did he say "deer"?

"Come on," he said. "Tide's going out, the current's pulling the boat away."

Kenzie adjusted her grip on the root. Still holding the animal by the collar, she tried to guide it toward the voice. It had stopped all resistance now and felt like a soggy stuffed toy.

"You're too far away," he said. "It might be easier if you opened your eyes."

"No. It burns like something's blinding me."

"Don't worry. It's just the salt water. It won't burn long."

Kenzie squeezed her eyes tighter.

"If you don't want her to drown, you've got to help me get her in the boat. Look, I can't do it alone."

Kenzie bit her lips in concentration. You can do this, she told herself. She cracked her eyes just long enough to aim. Then she let go of the ledge, touched both feet to the rocks, and shoved off. She felt a tug on the collar and realized that the current had carried her right to the boat.

"Okay, I've got her. Let go," he said.

The animal was lifted out of the water. Kenzie held on to the boat and pushed the hair out of her face.

"I'm going to pull you into the boat too," he said. "Open your eyes."

"Okay, but I won't like it."

"I don't think you're going to like it if you land on my fishing gear either. The hooks are sharp and the bait's slimy and stinky." He tugged on her arms. "Okay. Now, come on."

She boosted herself up and teetered on the side of the boat. He gripped her under the arms and pulled. Kenzie opened her eyes in time to gauge her fall and landed on a cushion instead of the dreaded fishhooks.

When she sat up she faced a lean, dark boy not much older

than herself. She couldn't see his eyes through his huge sunglasses, but the rest of his face was beaming.

She rubbed her eyes and blinked. He had said *deer.* The bedraggled animal lying in the boat between them wasn't a dog! It was a deer, the smallest deer she'd ever seen. It couldn't be more than a few weeks old. Why didn't it have spots?

"Good job," he said. "Looks like you got to her in time."

She barely heard the boy. The deer mesmerized her.

"Uh, nice of you to drop in," he said.

What's with the collar, she thought. Is it someone's pet?

"Hey, wake up." He poked her on the shoulder. "Are you okay? I'm Angelo. Who are you?"

"I'm sorry," she said. "I heard you, honest. Kenzie, my name's Kenzie and . . . ," she pointed, "that's a deer."

"No kidding. What'd you think it was, a cat?"

"Actually, I thought it was a dog."

He grinned and said, "It's a little doe. But it probably was a dog that chased her into the canal."

"She's so small." Kenzie lightly touched her fingers to the deer's wet neck.

"You thought she was a dog? For real?"

She nodded.

"You're a tourist, right?"

"I wish I were," she muttered. She hugged herself and shivered in spite of the sun's warmth.

"We've got to get going. It's a long way to the Refuge Center and this deer's in bad shape. Let's go." Angelo secured the oars, reached behind him, and started the little outboard.

"Wait! My mom's a nurse. Turn around. Go to the yellow house. She'll know what to do."

"You're sure?" he asked.

Kenzie nodded.

"Okay then." He put the motor in gear and swung the boat around. Keeping one hand on the tiller, he turned to face Kenzie.

Kenzie stroked the deer's sweet face and noticed the flicker of a long-lashed eyelid. She traced the black pattern, like the letter T, that stretched from the deer's nose to its eyes. The dark ears trimmed in white seemed far too large for such a tiny animal.

Kenzie shouted over the motor's rumble. "Angelo, why is she wearing a collar?"

"She's part of a scientific study. It's a radio collar."

"Is something wrong with her?"

He looked at the nearly lifeless deer and raised his eyebrows.

"Okay, that was silly," she said. "There's definitely something wrong with her now. I meant, well, she's so small. She must be a baby, but she doesn't have any spots. Is that normal?" Kenzie laid her hand on the little chest, willing it to continue rising.

"She's not a regular deer," he said. He leaned a little to see around Kenzie. "She's an endangered Florida Key deer."

"Really?! As in endangered species?"

"Yeah. The only place they live is Big Pine Key and a couple of nearby islands. All Key deer are small. A full-grown one is about the height of my German shepherd."

"So, she's not really a baby."

"She's lost her spots, but she's still pretty young."

"Gosh, I wonder how many are left."

"Scientists are counting them. They're all over the place here, though. They're totally tame."

Angelo cut the engine and the boat glided up to the dock. He grabbed a piling and wrapped the line around a cleat at the same time.

"When I get out, hold the boat," he said.

Kenzie steadied the boat. Angelo gathered the deer's limp little body in his strong arms. With his left arm under the deer's reddish brown rump and his right arm supporting its chest, he stepped up on the dock. Its petite head flopped on his shoulder.

Kenzie sloshed up the steps yelling, "Mom, Mom, are you up? Mom we need help!"

Angelo followed, cradling the deer.

Kenzie's mother rushed to the screen door, cell phone in hand. "Kenzie, what on earth?" Her eyes widened. "I have to go, Nana," she said. She put the phone on the counter and pushed the door open. "Kenzie, I was worried sick. What happened? You're sopping wet!" Suddenly she noticed Angelo holding the deer. "What's that?"

"A deer. We pulled it out of the canal. Do something!"

"But, who . . . how . . . ?"

"Mother!"

"Right. Okay." She rubbed her forehead and came out on the porch. "Kenzie, grab some of those towels off the kitchen table. Young man, put the poor thing here on the lounge chair, head at the low end."

Angelo gently positioned the deer and stepped back.

Kenzie's mother stooped down and studied the miniature deer. "It's no use." She slowly shook her head. "She's not . . ." She felt an area on the inside of the doe's dainty back leg. "Okay, there's a faint pulse. Well, maybe I could . . ." She looked up. "Oh boy, I've never ventilated a deer before, but why not? Kenzie, help me lay the little thing on its right side. Easy now."

Kenzie's mom opened the deer's jaws, carefully pulled its tongue forward, and placed her own mouth over the nose and mouth of the deer. She blew little puffs of air into its nostrils. The deer's tiny chest rose. She puffed again. Once more the chest rose.

Kenzie counted off one, two, three, four seconds for every puff her mother made. The little chest continued to rise and fall.

Finally, the little deer gurgled and coughed. She spit and began to quiver, staring at them with huge frightened brown eyes. As Kenzie and her mother dried the deer, it weakly flicked its black-tipped tail, exposing the white underside.

Kenzie's eyes filled. "I think we did it," she said. She turned, looking for Angelo. He was sitting on the corner of the porch rail. "Angelo, meet my mother, the miraculous Nurse Ryan."

He hopped down and joined them. "Wow, Ms. Ryan, you just saved an endangered species!"

She nodded. "This one was lucky."

"Guess we should call the Refuge Center," Angelo said. "They'll want to take her in for observation."

Kenzie stroked the deer's damp coat. Its dark eyes enchanted her. "Don't worry, little girl, you're going to be just fine. I'll be around to make sure of that."

The deer nudged her hand. She smiled, inhaled the tropical air, and wondered what other surprises awaited her on this astonishing island.

**Bonnie J. Doerr** *lives on a small island in the Florida Keys. She has lived in eight states and has taught a variety of subjects in as many grade levels. Currently, she teaches at Florida Keys Community College in Key West. Ms. Doerr has written poetry and nonfiction, and is working on a novel,* Kenzie's Golden Key.

# The Softshell Turtle

Steve Wilson

In water greened by algae, a green-shelled turtle hides

away. Afloat in brown plants, he is
a silence about which fish dart

and in the slow current the leaves of cabomba,
capillaried, sway like snakes. At rest, he is a stone
on the riverbed. He is invisible.

A suggestion, colored subtle as a lost coin.
Later, pulling the round illogic of his shape
up to nose the air of afternoons warmed by sun,

he rises. Light plays on the surface,
on his paddle feet, as he swims into sight,

offering me the moment of his coming.

**Steve Wilson***'s poetry has appeared in such journals as* America, Commonweal, *and* High Plains Literary Review. *He also has poems in the anthologies* American Poetry: The Next Generation, What Have You Lost?, *and* American Diaspora: Poetry of Displacement. *He lives in San Marcos, Texas.*

# The Ivory-Billed Woodpecker

JOHN JAMES AUDUBON

*The last official sighting of an ivory-billed woodpecker occurred in a Louisiana bottomland forest in 1944, just as the forest was being cleared. In recent years a few people have claimed to see an ivory-billed woodpecker, but there have been no substantiated reports. Reading this nineteenth-century account by naturalist and artist John James Audubon, one understands the urge to remain hopeful that ivory-bills, known as the King of the Woodpeckers, still reign over some secluded patch of forest.*

The Ivory-billed Woodpecker confines its rambles to a comparatively very small portion of the United States, it never having been observed in the Middle States within the memory of any person now living there. In fact, in no portion of these districts does the nature of the woods appear suitable to its remarkable habits.

Descending the Ohio, we meet with this splendid bird for the first time near the confluence of that beautiful river and the Mississippi; after which, following the windings of the latter, either downwards toward the sea, or upwards in the direction of the Missouri, we frequently observe it. On the Atlantic coast, North Carolina may be taken as the limit of its distribution, although now and then an individual of the species may be accidentally seen in Maryland. To the westward of the

Mississippi, it is found in all the dense forests bordering the streams which empty their waters into that majestic river, from the very declivities of the Rocky Mountains. The lower parts of the Carolinas, Georgia, Alabama, Louisiana, and Mississippi, are, however, the most favourite resorts of this bird, and in those States it constantly resides, breeds, and passes a life of peaceful enjoyment, finding a profusion of food in all the deep, dark, and gloomy swamps dispersed throughout them.

I wish, kind reader, it were in my power to present to your mind's eye the favourite resort of the Ivory-billed Woodpecker. Would that I could describe the extent of those deep morasses, overshadowed by millions of gigantic dark cypresses, spreading their sturdy moss-covered branches, as if to admonish intruding man to pause and reflect on the many difficulties which he must encounter, should he persist in venturing farther into their almost inaccessible recesses, extending for miles before him, where he should be interrupted by huge projecting branches, here and there the massy trunk of a fallen and decaying tree, and thousands of creeping and twining plants of numberless species! Would that I could represent to you the dangerous nature of the ground, its oozing, spongy, and miry disposition, although covered with a beautiful but treacherous carpeting, composed of the richest mosses, flags, and water-lilies, no sooner receiving the pressure of the foot than it yields and endangers the very life of the adventurer, whilst here and there, as he approaches an opening, that proves merely a lake of black muddy water, his ear is assailed by the dismal croaking of innumerable frogs, the hissing of serpents, or the bellowing of alligators! Would that I could give you an idea of the sultry pestiferous atmosphere that nearly suffocates the intruder during the meridian heat of our dogdays, in those gloomy and horrible swamps! But the attempt to picture these scenes would be vain. Nothing short of ocular demonstration can impress any adequate idea of them. . . .

The flight of this bird is graceful in the extreme, although seldom prolonged to more than a few hundred yards at a time, unless when it has to cross a large river, which it does in deep undulations, opening its wings at first to their full extent, and nearly closing them to renew the propelling impulse. The transit from one tree to another, even should the distance be as much as a hundred yards, is performed by a single sweep, and the bird appears as if merely swinging itself from the top of the one tree to that of the other, forming an elegantly curved line. At this moment all the beauty of the plumage is exhibited, and strikes the beholder with pleasure. It never utters any sound whilst on wing, unless during the love season; but at all other times, no sooner has this bird alighted than its remarkable voice is heard, at almost every leap which it makes, whilst ascending against the upper parts of the trunk of a tree, or its highest branches. Its notes are clear, loud, and yet rather plaintive. They are heard at a considerable distance, perhaps half a mile, and resemble the false high note of a clarionet. They are usually repeated three times in succession, and may be represented by the monosyllable *pait, pait, pait.* These are heard so frequently as to induce me to say that the bird spends few minutes of the day without uttering them, and this circumstance leads to its destruction, which is aimed at, not because (as is supposed by some) this species is a destroyer of trees, but more because it is a beautiful bird, and its rich scalp attached to the upper mandible forms an ornament for the war-dress of most of our Indians, or for the shot-pouch of our squatters and hunters, by all of whom the bird is shot merely for that purpose. . . .

The Ivory-billed Woodpecker nestles earlier in spring than any other species of its tribe. I have observed it boring a hole for that purpose in the beginning of March. The hole is, I believe, always made in the trunk of a live tree, generally an ash or a hagberry, and is at a great height. The birds pay great regard to the particular situation of the tree, and the inclination of its trunk; first, because they prefer retirement, and again, because they are anxious to secure the aperture against the access of water during beating rains. To prevent such a calamity, the hole is generally dug immediately under the junction of a large branch with the trunk. It is first bored horizontally for a few inches, then directly downwards, and not in a spiral manner, as some people have imagined. According to circumstances, this cavity is more or less deep, being sometimes not more than ten inches, whilst at other times it reaches nearly three feet downwards into the core of the tree. I have been led to think that these differences result from the more or less immediate necessity under which the female may be of depositing her eggs, and again have thought that the older the Woodpecker is, the deeper does it make its hole. The average diameter of the different nests which I have examined was about seven inches within, although the entrance, which is perfectly round, is only just large enough to admit the bird.

Both birds work most assiduously at this excavation, one waiting outside to encourage the other, whilst it is engaged in digging, and when the latter is fatigued, taking its place. I have approached trees whilst these Woodpeckers were thus busily employed in forming their nest, and by resting my head against the bark, could easily distinguish every blow given by the bird. I observed that in two instances, when the Woodpeckers saw me thus at the foot of the tree in which they were digging their nest, they abandoned it for ever. For the first brood there are generally six eggs. They are deposited on a few chips at the bottom of the hole, and are of a pure white colour. The young are seen creeping out of the hole about a fortnight before they venture to fly to any other tree. The second brood makes its appearance about the 15th of August. . . .

This species generally moves in pairs, after the young have left their parents. The female is always the most clamorous and the least shy. Their mutual attachment is, I believe, continued through life. Excepting when digging a hole for the reception of their eggs, these birds seldom, if ever, attack living trees, for any other purpose than that of procuring food, in doing which they destroy the insects that would otherwise prove injurious to the trees.

I have frequently observed the male and female retire to rest for the night, into the same hole in which they had long before reared their young. This generally happens a short time after sunset.

When wounded and brought to the ground, the Ivory-bill immediately makes for the nearest tree, and ascends it with great rapidity and perseverance, until it reaches the top branches, when it squats and hides, generally with great effect. Whilst ascending, it moves spirally round the tree, utters its loud *pait, pait, pait,* at almost every hop, but becomes silent the moment it reaches a place where it conceives itself secure. They sometimes cling to the bark with their claws so firmly, as to remain cramped to the spot for several hours after death.

When taken by the hand, which is rather a hazardous undertaking, they strike with great violence, and inflict very severe wounds with their bill as well as claws, which are extremely sharp and strong. On such occasions, this bird utters a mournful and very piteous cry.

*A dedicated naturalist,* **John James Audubon** *studied, painted, and wrote about the wildlife of North America. Among his many published works are* Birds of America *(1827),* Quadrupeds of North America *(1849), and* Ornithological Biography *(1831), from which this excerpt is taken.*

# Eulogy for a Hermit Crab

PATTIANN ROGERS

You were consistently brave
On these surf-drenched rocks, in and out of their salty
Slough holes around which the entire expanse
Of the glinting grey sea and the single spotlight
Of the sun went spinning and spinning and spinning
In a tangle of blinding spume and spray
And pistol-shot collisions your whole life long.
You stayed. Even with the wet icy wind of the moon
Circling your silver case night after night after night
You were here.

And by the gritty orange curve of your claws,
By the soft, wormlike grip
Of your hinter body, by the unrelieved wonder
Of your black-pea eyes, by the mystified swing
And swing and swing of your touching antennae,
You maintained your name meticulously, you kept
Your name intact exactly, day after day after day.
No one could say you were less than perfect
In the hermitage of your crabness.

Now, beside the racing, incomprehensible racket
Of the sea stretching its great girth forever

Back and forth between this direction and another,
Please let the words of this proper praise I speak
Become the identical and proper sound
Of my mourning.

**Pattiann Rogers** *has published seven books of poetry, including* Firekeeper: New and Selected Poems *and, most recently,* Song of the World Becoming: New and Collected Poems 1981–2001. *She lived for many years near Houston and now makes her home in Colorado.*

# Swimming with Mermaids

## Charles Bergman

*Manatees, sometimes called sea cows, are large, plant-eating mammals that inhabit rivers and coastal areas of the Gulf Coast region. These creatures are so docile that people can safely swim in their company. Too many human visitors, especially ones who are insensitive to the manatees' needs for space and tranquility, can disturb the gentle creatures. But under the best of circumstances, spending time with these endangered animals can be a profound and transforming experience.*

She touched me with a sudden, unexpected intimacy. A large manatee, she had been sculling across the bright limestone bottom of Crystal River, in Florida, near the springs that feed the pellucid waters of the manatee sanctuary. When she saw me above her, she plumped slowly to the surface like a dirigible, rotating indolently to face me, seeming to linger through each movement. I braced for the encounter.

Her approach was slow—an infinitely sweet, infinitely guileless address. She looked vaguely like a walrus, with her flat, whiskered nose and duffel-bag body. Her truncated snout and large, prehensile lips revealed some of her distant and ancient relation to the elephant. Her skin, gray and leathery, reminded me in its roughness of a cracked ceramic plate. Sunk deep into her face, her pinprick eyes seemed much too small for her immense bulk. She looked out at me from within a blubberous body, through the bleary film over her eyes.

Except in a spectacularly homely way, you could not call her beautiful. Funny, then, that manatees were most likely the creatures that early sailors mistook for mermaids. But her trust and openness were irresistible, endearing. As she paddled the water with her splayed flippers, I could see the bones moving beneath the skin like the fingers inside a child's mitten. On her skin, short and delicate hairs wavered in the water. Manatees are tactile creatures. They love to touch, and these sparse hairs increase the manatee's sensitivity.

She treaded toward me, within inches of my face. Still, I was not prepared for what she did. With a gentle and startling thud, she banged into my face mask with her bristled snout. It was as surprising as a first kiss, and just as memorable.

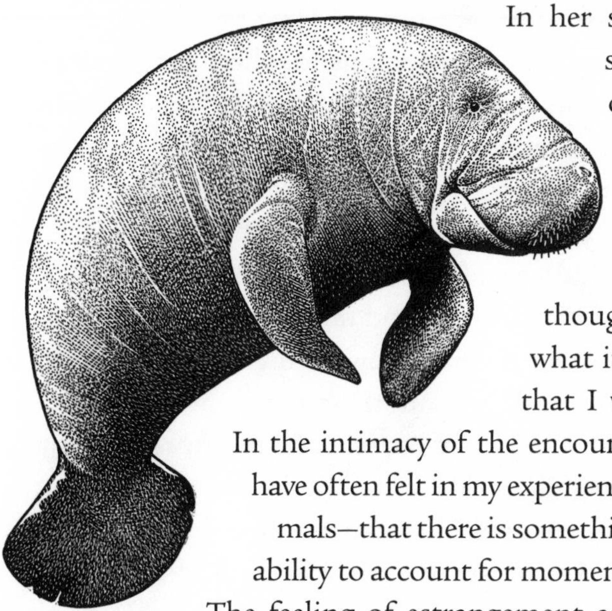

This manatee had come toward me like an idea taking shape. In her steady approach, she became an increasingly significant presence. She evoked in me a powerful desire for more, though I could not tell what it was at the time that I wanted more of. In the intimacy of the encounter, I felt what I have often felt in my experiences with wild animals—that there is something lacking in our ability to account for moments like these. The feeling of estrangement and the desire to know nature grow with the awareness of the loss of nature in our time. I had come to the Crystal River to study manatees as part of the research for my book on endangered animals. Swimming with this manatee gave me a sense for how I might begin to create new kinds of relationships with animals. I do not think we can ever know other creatures completely, but I do believe we can achieve relationships richer in intimacy and intensity than those we are now capable of.

Usually, with wild animals, I am a spectator, watching them from a distance. With this manatee in the Crystal River, however, I was in her element, swimming with her in a slow-motion process of discovery. I must have been a comical sight: my cheeks squished inside a face mask and my lips almost orange on a cold winter morning. She seemed to like peering at me. Bound in a mutual gaze, we floated together in the water, mask to massive snout.

Even though manatees are famous for their gentleness, I confess I felt uncomfortable. Through my face mask, I could see only a small circumference, in a kind of tunnel vision. The manatee started to drift to the left, inspecting me. Her hulking and harmless being seemed at peace in the warm waters, like a gentle sea-Buddha, and her motions were elegant in their simple, casual drift. With her round tail flipper, big as a manhole cover, she propelled herself toward my left, behind me. With a hint of panic I found myself sculling almost frenetically to keep her within the narrow field of view afforded by my face mask. I bent myself in contortions at the waist to keep facing her, kicking stupidly, absurdly, with my flippers. But I could not match her moves in the water. I started to lose sight of her as she slid behind my back. I did not want her behind me.

Something about her unguarded easiness made me feel slightly ashamed. I suddenly felt tyrannized by this need to see.

It was a strange moment. The recollection of being in the water, straining to keep an utterly innocuous manatee within the frame and periphery of my face mask, has stayed with me. I continue to mull the disquiet I felt in the encounter. I have come to believe that the nervousness I felt while swimming with this manatee was related to my need to *see* her, because that is how we have learned to relate to animals—largely through the eyes.

But the same manatee also showed me how my experience of animals might be enlarged. It was an unusually cool day on the Crystal River. Steam played over the surface of the cloud-darkened river. The slack drift of the waters had a hypnotic, almost narcotic tranquility to it. While the manatee swam in her slow career around me, I tried to open myself to this creature, tried to imagine how she must experience the world.

Almost everything we know about manatees appeals to that part of us that longs for a peaceful, unhurried approach to life. Once, she settled toward the bottom, as if luxuriating in these warm waters, and then rose again with an effortless buoyancy. Breaking the surface with just her nose, she sent up a swoosh of breath in a small feathery spray. I got the feeling that she moved not through water but through the medium of a dream, swimming in a kind of aquatic somnambulance. I could not help but wonder what notions, flitting like fish through the streams of her thought, were able to curl her lips in such a self-satisfied smile.

I stayed in the water for over an hour. I felt changed by the manatee as I swam with her. She embarrassed me out of my sense of superiority. Although she was homely, her appearance mattered less and less the longer I was with her in the water. I quit struggling to watch her, and we just drifted. She swung around behind me and banged into my back with the tender thump of fifteen hundred pounds. She nuzzled my sides and chest with her nose, as if she were smelling me. She seemed to want to know me through smell and feel.

I like to think of myself as the author of my own experience—as if my life were a story that I am writing. But with the manatee, there could be no illusion that I was the author of the encounter. This was her drama, and my role was unfolding as I took part. She dived below me, came up, and bumped into my belly. She rolled over, sinking. Then, like a huge and slowly spinning bubble, she bobbed toward me again and nudged my side. Wafting her flat, round tail, she spiked toward the bottom, where she tumbled onto her back with an elephantine magnificence. In her superbly languid torpor, she rose toward me once more, coming at me from an angle with all her engaging, unpretentious bulk. Her face was eloquent with curiosity, playfulness, and the serene vulnerability of things that simply are what they are.

**Charles Bergman** *is the author of* Wild Echoes: Encounters with the Most Endangered Animals in North America *(McGraw-Hill, 1990) and* Orion's Legacy: A Cultural History of Man as Hunter *(Dutton, 1996), and is widely published in magazines such as* Orion, Smithsonian, Audubon, *and* Natural History. *He loves animals deeply, and the animals themselves—like the manatee in this story—have taught him what it means to love the world.*

# Alligator Crossing

## Marjory Stoneman Douglas

*In her novel* Alligator Crossing, *Marjory Stoneman Douglas tells the story of a troubled teenager from Miami who ventures into the Everglades by hiding on the boat of an alligator poacher named Dillon. Once discovered, Henry comes to appreciate Dillon's knowledge of the Everglades, although he never loses his loathing of the man's occupation. In this excerpt from the novel, Henry briefly leaves Dillon to paddle a boat around a secluded stretch of Everglades National Park.*

The flat boat was buoyant with emptiness. Henry shoved it off and stood for a moment with the paddle in his hand, his face turned to the sky. He was completely, entirely, utterly alone. When he looked around him at the green leaves on the pond, the water rippling in the wind that bent the tall yellow grasses beyond the nearer shore, he had in his life never been so filled with sheer, mindless, unutterable delight.

The white birds they had disturbed were feeding again by the farther shore. Two pink birds flew over. They flew with their necks straight, sticking out funny-shaped bills, wonderful pink birds with deep rosy splashes on their wings. Spoonbill—roseate spoonbill, he thought before he realized it. He was so excited because he had recognized them from the pictures that he nearly fell overboard. Birds—gallinules that he remembered, and coots—were clucking among the lily pads. Overhead a buzzard tilted its black wings and, motionless, rode high up a mounting column of air. There were fish in the water around him, long gray shapes. He thought they were garfish that somebody said the Indians ate.

Presently, full to the brim with happiness, he sat down in the stern and practiced paddling. He got half across. Then he saw a bird and forgot to paddle. It was sitting, black and tan, on one of the scrubby bushes at the water's edge. It had a long snaky neck like those cormorants in the Bay of Florida, but

this was longer. It was the snakebird, he remembered. Dillon called it a "water turkey." He waited, perfectly still, and saw the bird dip easily from its branch in a long dive to the water—down into it and disappear. It was swimming down there in the dim weedy water, with the little fish darting. He waited and waited to see it come up, but he couldn't tell if it was that one or another that came flying over and took to another tree.

Everywhere he looked he could see birds, paddling at the water's edge, hanging on the farther reeds, chirring or flying over low and busy, standing on long legs in the shallows, like a heron over there with its long sharp beak extended like a lance at the ready. Up there higher in the sky, birds crisscrossed it with wings floating, turning, dipping or soaring high—high up like the buzzard, swinging on the point of one black wing right against the dazzling breast of a cloud rising up snowy into the sun.

When he brought his eyes down they were swimming with too much light. It was as if, from this moment, he wanted never to move again.

When his eyes cleared he saw two dark bumps of alligator eyes and a smaller bump of a nose moving easily out from among the lily pads. It was only a little distance between the eyes. The easy swirl of water behind was the sculling ridgy tail. It wasn't a big alligator, only about two foot and a half, about the size of George. He kept perfectly still as it went by, cocking an eye at his shadow. The curving mouth smiled a little. The short front legs hung down foolishly by the bulge of the body. It was just a small blackish alligator moving across a pond, just where he belonged—probably looking for a turtle to crunch on from the other side.

Henry thought about it slowly. Thinking was hard.

Everything that lived here—the alligator, the little fish and big fish, the turtles, the frogs, the dragonflies—lived on something else alive that was here, even the green water plants in the clear brown water. There seemed to be enough for them all so long as there was enough fresh water. Only the alligator was not killed and eaten by anything—except man. But man was different. Man frightened Henry, but not these strange bright living things as intensely alive as he was.

It was so—so nice here. If he could only stay here by himself. It was impossible. There were all the things a boy had to face, just growing up. It looked hard to him in this moment of peace. Yet he had lived through a lot of things already, he remembered suddenly, as if his life before this was already a long time ago. He was still astonished that he had found his way to this. The idea came to him slowly that perhaps there were things as fine as this waiting for him somewhere, that he could not imagine now. He had a new, strong sense of hope that was not a boy's imagining.

**Marjory Stoneman Douglas,** *a passionate defender of the Everglades, lived in Florida from 1915 until her death in 1998, at the age of 108. She wrote numerous articles, short stories, and books in which Florida served as either setting or subject, including her most famous book,* The Everglades: River of Grass.

# Migration Midpoint: What We Can See from Here

DAVID WILLIAMS

We can't see the warm,
rising spirals of air
these monarch butterflies ride,

or their caterpillar selves filled up
with leaves of silk-thread milkweed
way back in New Brunswick,

or the dense, silk drapes
their gathering will make
in the firs of Michoacan.

From here, we can see
their wind-torn, stubborn
lines joined by one desire—

to fulfill the journey
and set out fresh,
as they have since

long before we scratched
our claims on sky and earth.
Fragile, essential, monarchs pass

reflected in your fresh eyes.
We hear wings in your voice
when you whisper

*Look!*

**David Williams** *is the author of* Traveling Mercies *(Alice James Books). His work is anthologized in* Poetry from the Amicus Journal, *edited by Peter Borelli and Brian Swann (Natural Resources Defense Council), and* What Have You Lost? *edited by Naomi Shihab Nye (Greenwillow/Macmillan).*

# The Dead Shark

ZIPORAH HILDEBRANDT

*Many people who fish or swim in the Gulf of Mexico feel a great fear of sharks, forgetting, of course, who the top predator in the Gulf Coast region really is.*

Many summers when I was young, I traveled with my father to visit my grandmother in her little pink stucco saltbox at the north end of Anna Maria Island. My grandparents had built their dreamhouse in the Florida "jungle," but by the time I came along my grandfather and the jungle were both gone. My grandmother was an artist. Mandalas of shells and starfish hung on the walls, with paintings of flowers, animals, and wild Florida rivers—the wilder the better. My grandma and I loved fierce, wild creatures.

From my grandmother's living room I could look across the sandy road over the dunes, to watch the sunset over the Gulf. That beach stretched forever, and there was never anybody on it but us. My father fished while I swam or played in the sand. When my grandmother came with us, I helped her pick over shells as she complained that the good ones were all gone. She wouldn't let me in the water because of sharks.

Every morning my father and I walked along the empty road to the fishing pier. My breath came quick as I walked way out over the water on those old gray boards. There were no railings, just the pilings the pier was built on jutting up for the birds. Pelicans and gulls waited there for someone to clean a fish, then they raced to be first to get the pieces. I loved the laughing gulls' cry, which started quick and fierce but trailed off sadly.

Everyone at the pier knew my father. He had been fishing in Florida since he was twenty-some years old, learning to be a pilot in the war. He knew every kind of fish, every shell and bird. He always bought some bait and settled on a folding chair with a can of beer. I liked lifting the thin boards covering the bait tanks to peer in at the squid glittering like stars in the shadowy water.

I was shy around the other fishermen and women. I brought my pole one day. I wanted to sit beside my father in the shade, but all the chairs were taken. I sat on the other side, away from the cigarettes, where it was quieter.

I curled a shrimp along the hook the way I'd learned, and tossed it the long way down to the water. I let some line run out. Fishing takes patience, so I sat still, waiting for the tug on my line that meant a fish was nibbling on my bait. Every once in a while I turned the handle on my reel, pulling the line in just a tiny bit, slowly, so the fish would think the shrimp was sort of sleepy. Mm, what kind of fish would I catch? Maybe a cobia—my father's favorite—or a red snapper, my grandma's.

My back was heating up. My eyes got tired from the dazzling patterns the sun traced on the waves. When someone walked by, their footsteps jarred from the planks to the inside of my head. Terns hovered over a school of tiny fish, dipping down fast and up again, slivers of silver wriggling in their beaks. The snaky neck of a cormorant disappeared into the dark green water. I brought my line in another inch, waiting for the cormorant to reappear. There it was, way over by the breakwater. Footsteps thudded on the boards and stopped right behind me. I tried to be polite and look around to say hello, but my neck was stiff from sitting still.

"Fishing for balloon fish?" The man laughed loudly.

"What?" I said. I'd never heard of balloon fish, but I wouldn't mind catching one.

He laughed again, and pointed over the edge.

Something about the way he did it made me feel cold, like an ice cube was sliding down my back. I leaned over to look.

There was my empty hook, dangling in the air halfway between the water and the dock. Heat rushed over me. I cranked the line in as fast as I could.

The man walked away, still laughing.

I was more careful where I fished after that. If there was anybody trying for balloon fish, I wanted to be the only one who knew about it.

One day Bob, one of the regulars, caught a skate. We gathered around as it flopped and smacked the deck, standing away from its flailing tail. The skin was smooth and brown on top, like sunlit gravel in a mountain brook, and I thought it must hurt it to lie on that splintery dry wood. Frank, the pier owner, flipped it over and I saw its weird white belly. It gave me the same queasy feeling I got when I turned over a rock with pale grubs and centipedes squirming underneath, ants scurrying to grab their eggs.

"What are you going to do with it?" Frank asked Bob.

"Throw it back, I guess. You want it?"

"Yep. I can use some shark bait."

Frank went to his shed and came out with the biggest

fishhook I'd ever seen. Longer than my forearm, it was as big around as three of my fingers. Instead of a wire leader, it had a sturdy chain that Frank tied on to a rope. He hitched the other end of the rope around a tall piling at the corner of the pier, by the crane and winch. He took the big knife from the sheath on his belt and slashed the skate's belly, then plunged that huge hook into the hole he'd made. With a heave, the bloody skate—now dead, I hoped—splashed off the deep end of the pier.

The next morning when my father and I got there, an eight-foot nurse shark hung from the winch above the pier.

Nobody did much fishing that morning. Everybody stood around drinking beer, smoking cigarettes, and looking at the shark. Everyone who came to the pier heard the story and joined us. A photographer from the newspaper took pictures for the front page.

What is it about sharks? Everyone talked and talked about that dead one hanging there. I was just as fascinated. I had never seen such a big, dead creature. I wanted to touch it but I got scared when my father held me back. "I thought it was dead," I said. l," he assured me. But no one else got close, either.

Death drew us and held us. I could picture those jagged teeth taking off my arm or my leg, even my head, the gaping mouth swallowing, sucking my father under the waves. Oh, it gave me *shivers.*

But scaring myself, the way my friends and I scared ourselves with creepy stories after midnight, seemed to dishonor the shark. It was just living its life when it swallowed that hook, not looking for trouble or revenge. I felt sorry for it, and sorry for the skate that lured the shark to a death as horrible as any suffered by humans from sharks.

Were the others thinking that, too? Wondering when it's right to kill and whether animals' feelings matter? I couldn't tell. Maybe they were, but they hid their thoughts under jokes and scorn, the way bullies on the playground made fun of a boy before they beat him up.

When we went to the pier the next day, the shark was gone. "What happened to it?" I asked.

"Oh, he probably cut it up for bait, or threw it back," my father told me.

Back to the sea, to the belly of another fish, another shark. As though the sea could swallow anything a person threw in, everything people didn't want or couldn't use.

**Ziporah Hildebrandt** *writes, gardens, and enjoys nature, mostly in Massachusetts. She likes science fiction, cross-country skiing, and writing to elected officials on behalf of endangered species. Her most recent book, a biography for young people, is about Brazilian senator Marina Silva, rain forest activist.*

# Manatee

## JILL BARRIE

Globular, whiskered, flat-tailed,
and flippered, in sunny green shallows
where sea grasses grow, you graze
in the shadow of propeller boats,
monofilament line, flat-bottomed barges
that skim the sea floor, insensible
to your presence. Defenseless, myopic,
in groups or alone, you migrate
to slow-moving rivers, natural springs,
or industrial outflows to winter.
We study the scars striating your skin.
You swim beside our canoe,
your squeaks and squeals unintelligible
to us, though your message is clear:
*We are here, we are here . . .*

**Jill Barrie** *has written poems off and on for more than twenty years. Although she currently lives in the middle of the country, one of her favorite places to visit is the Gulf Coast of Florida.*

# Alabama Dreaming

EDWARD O. WILSON

*Most people would be repelled by the idea of tromping through a swamp teeming with poisonous snakes. But for a boy of fifteen, fascinated by the variety and wildness of life on Earth, few places were more exciting and enticing.*

In August 1944 I weighed 112 pounds. I know this to be true because in that month I reported with my best friend, Philip Bradley, for football practice at Brewton High School, and we were put on the scales in the locker room. At fifteen years, I was probably the youngest, and certainly the smallest, of the players. Bradley was a bit heavier, at 116 pounds, every ounce of which I envied, while the largest member of the team came in at a hulking 160 pounds. I was allowed to strap on my ridiculously oversized uniform because the team needed every man (well, every boy) it could get. And I was there despite my obvious lack of qualifications because this was Alabama. In small towns across the state, football was what young males between the ages of fifteen and nineteen aspired to do when not in class or occupied with part-time jobs. At the other end of the statistical curve of athletic promise from me, boys with heavy shoulders and quick hands could hope for college athletic scholarships.

There happened to be, however, none in our school well enough endowed for college play that year.

Brewton was and still is a town of about five thousand on the Alabama side of the border with Florida, forty miles north of Pensacola. It has changed very little since 1944. I have returned twice in middle age while on my way by automobile across the state, to drift like a phantom through the grid of residential streets down to the main commercial section that runs parallel to the railroad tracks, and to pause at the grounds of the high school, where I summoned the memory of boys hitting the worn tackle bag, grunting, and joking back and forth in reasonably close imitations of grown men. Once I stopped to ask a young fireman for directions, and when I mentioned that I had attended the high school in 1944, he said, "Boy, that was a l-o-o-ng time ago!" I replied that it didn't seem very long to me, not in a pleasant little town that had conceded so little to the rush of the twentieth century. And not when I could close my eyes and summon uniforms caked with dried mud and turned aromatic by stale sweat.

There were twenty-three on the football squad that year, composing the first and second teams of eleven each, each member playing both offense and defense, plus me, the third-string left end and, by accident of numbers, the entire third string. I couldn't catch the football half the time, I couldn't even see a pass coming with my one good eye, and I was too light to block. About all I could manage was a shoestring tackle. If I dived to the ground and threw my arms around both ankles of the onrushing ball carrier, I could trip him, hoping he wouldn't fall onto me too hard. Somehow, perhaps because the opposing teams were even punier than our own, we managed to defeat every one of the other ten high schools we played except archrival Greenville. I was allowed on the field just once all season, in the fourth quarter of the final game, played at home, and this once because it was toward the end of the fourth quarter and the enemy had been crushed beyond all hope of recovery. How warmly I remember and cherish the command, "Wilson, take left end!" It was an act of charity on the part of the coach, whose name I have forgotten but toward whom I will always feel gratitude. Because of him I was thereafter authorized to say in that part of Alabama, "I played football for Brewton," in the same way a New York corporate executive in a Century Club dining room says, "I rowed for Yale."

Most of the players had nicknames such as Bubba (it was not a joke then; Bubbas were future good old boys and managers of Chevrolet dealerships; they were big, heavyset, and good-natured), J. C., Buddy, Skeeter, Scooter, and Shoe. Mine was Snake, not because of my body shape, which would have been apropos, and certainly not because I could weave magically through crowds of tacklers head down with the ball tucked hard on my waist, as in my dreams, but because I had maintained my enthusiasm for real snakes. After our sojourn in Mobile, my father had left me with Belle Raub in Pensacola and gone on the road with Pearl, to a destination I never knew. The three of us reunited in a small house in Brewton in the early spring of 1944. That summer I served as Boy Scout nature counselor at Camp Bigheart, on the shore of Pensacola Bay. Once again I relied on snakes to enliven accounts of natural history.

By this time reptiles and amphibians had become my central interest. The fauna of the region would excite passion in a herpetologist of any age. Forty species of snakes, one of the richest assemblages in the world, are native to the western Florida panhandle and adjacent border counties of Alabama. Over a period of a year I managed to capture most of them. And a majority of those I could not take alive I either saw at a distance, such as the marsh-dwelling flat-tailed water snake *(Natrix compressicauda),* or else were brought to me dead, most memorably a large diamondback rattlesnake killed by a group of men not far from our house.

On the western edge of Brewton, next to a dense swamp, was a goldfish hatchery run by an affable sixty-year-old Englishman named Mr. Perry. I never learned his first name; polite southern youth did not address their elders in such familiar terms. Nor did I ask him how he came to such an unusual occupation in a backwater southern town. But we became good friends and spent hours talking freely on many subjects. He was always glad to see me when I rode my bicycle up to the edge of the property. He never had other visitors that I saw, lived quietly with his wife in a small house on the property, and always worked alone. His water came from artesian wells that have since dried up, and he fed his goldfish cornmeal mixed with pig blood received weekly from a local slaughterhouse. The goldfish were sold for bait, both locally and out of town. His canisters of young fish, some monochromatic gold, others gold marbled with white, departed at regular intervals by rail from the Brewton station.

Perry had excavated the ponds, each twenty to thirty feet square, in an irregular double row along the edge of the swamp. Thick weeds choked their borders, and tall trees walled them in on the swamp side. A six-foot-wide stream of artesian water flowed into the swamp from each end of the hatchery. The whole ensemble was a textbook diagram from an ecology textbook made literal: the rich nutrients pumped in continuously gave birth to an exuberance of algae, aquatic plants, and fish. The net produce of biomass fed swarms of insects and thence of frogs, snakes, herons, and other larger predators; and all the excess food and all the waste draining into the exit streams fructified the biota of a deep swamp that stretched east for an indeterminate distance.

Into this paradise I threw myself with abandon. The hours I spent there were among the happiest of my life. At every opportunity I came down to the hatchery ponds. After talking with Mr. Perry for a while, mostly about his pisciculture and my own explorations, I donned calf-length rubber boots from the row of pairs he kept in his equipment shed and walked into my private world. At home I politely ignored the nagging of my stepmother, who seemed almost distraught at my failure to find a job after school. I in turn grew increasingly abashed and resentful at her singleminded efforts to prepare me for the grim Depression-era life she had experienced. I had already worked longer hours than she, I had proved myself, and now I needed space. Pearl saw little value in my swamp expeditions, and, looking back, I cannot blame her.

Adults forget the depths of languor into which the adolescent mind descends with ease. They are prone to undervalue the mental growth that occurs during daydreaming and aimless wandering. When I focused on the ponds and swamp lying before me, I abandoned all sense of time. Net in hand, khaki collecting satchel hung by a strap from my shoulder, I surveilled the edges of the ponds, poked shrubs and grass clumps, and occasionally waded out into shallow stretches of open water to stir the muddy bottom. Often I just sat for long periods scanning the pond edges and vegetation for the hint of a scaly coil, a telltale ripple on the water's surface, the sound of an out-of-sight splash. Then, sooner on hot days than otherwise, I worked my way down for a half-mile or so along one of the effluent streams into the deep shade of the swamp, crossed through the forest to the parallel stream, and headed back up it to the hatchery. Sometimes I cut away to explore pools and mudflats hidden in the Piranesian gloom beneath the high closed canopy. In the swamp I was a wanderer in a miniature wilderness. I never encountered another person there, never heard a distant voice, or automobile, or airplane. The only tracks in the mud I saw were those of wild animals. No one else cared about this domain, not even Mr. Perry. Although I held no title, the terrain and its treasures belonged entirely to me in every sense that mattered.

Water snakes abounded at abnormally high densities around the ponds and along the outflow streams, feeding on schools of blood-gorged fish and armies of frogs. Mr. Perry made no attempt to control them. They were, he said, no more than a minor source of goldfish mortality. Although neither of us had the vocabulary to express such things, we shared the concept of a balanced ecosystem, one in which man could add and take out energy but otherwise leave alone without ill consequence. Mr. Perry was a natural-born environmentalist. He trod lightly upon the land in his care.

A swamp filled with snakes may be a nightmare to most, but for me it was a ceaselessly rotating lattice of wonders. I had the same interest in the diversity of snakes that other fifteen-year-old boys seemed automatically to develop in the years and makes of automobiles. And knowing them well, I had no fear. On each visit I found something new. I captured live specimens, brought them home to cages I had constructed of wood and wire mesh, and fed them frogs and minnows I collected at the hatchery.

My favorites included the eastern ribbon snakes, graceful reptiles decorated with green and brown longitudinal stripes, which spent their time draped in communal bunches on tree limbs overhanging the pond waters. With their bulging, lidless eyes they could see at a considerable distance and were wary. I stalked them to within a few feet by wading in the shallow water of the pond edges and seized one or two at a time as they plunged into the water and tried to swim away. They grew tame in captivity and fed readily on small frogs. Green water snakes were memorable in another way. Found lying half-concealed in vegetation at the edge of the ponds, they were big, up to four feet in length, and heavy-bodied. Catching one was an unpleasant experience unless I could take them quickly back of the head. Most larger snakes try to bite when first handled, and many can break the skin to leave a horseshoe row of needle pricks; but green water snakes have an especially violent response, and their sharp teeth can slash the skin and make blood run freely. They were also difficult to maintain in captivity. Once I found a mud snake, a species that uses the hardened tip of its tail to help hold giant amphiuma salamanders while subduing and swallowing them. The tip can prick human skin; hence the species' alternate name of stinging snake.

One species, the glossy watersnake *Natrix rigida,* became a special target just because it was so elusive. The small adults lay on the bottom of shallow ponds well away from the shore and pointed their heads out of the alga-green water in order to breathe and scan the surface in all directions. I waded out to them very slowly, avoiding the abrupt lateral movements to which reptiles are most sensitive. I needed to get within three or four feet in order to dive and grab them by the body, but before I could close the distance they always pulled their heads under and slipped quietly away into the deeper, opaque waters. I finally solved the problem with the aid of the town's leading slingshot artist, a taciturn loner my age who liked me because I praised his skills as a hunter. He aimed pebbles at the heads of the snakes with surprising accuracy, stunning several long enough for me to seize them underwater. After they recovered, I kept the captives for a while in the homemade cages, where they thrived on live minnows offered in dishes of water.

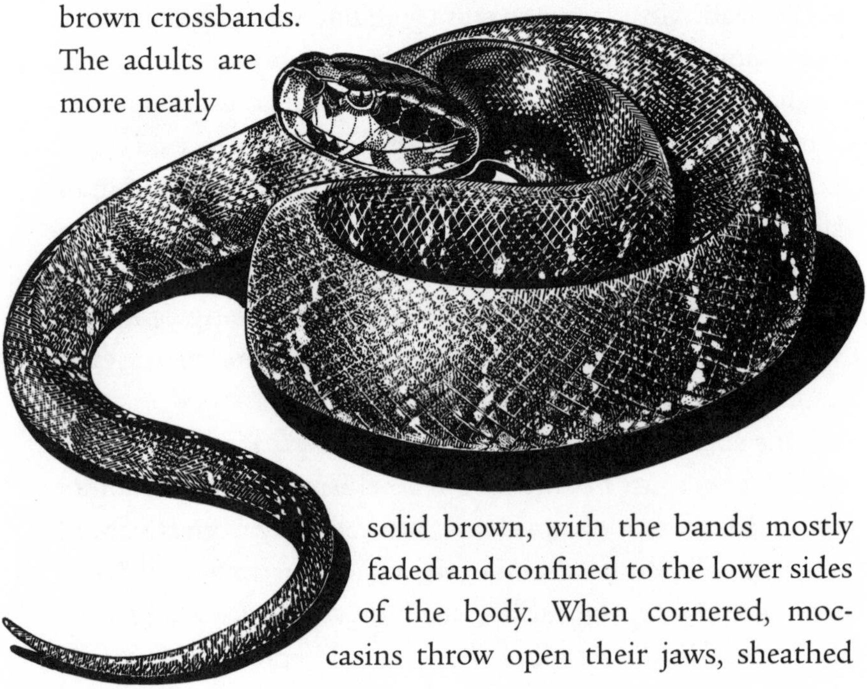

The tigers and lords of this place were the poisonous cottonmouth moccasins, large semiaquatic pit vipers with thick bodies and triangular heads. Young individuals, measuring eighteen inches or so, are brightly patterned with reddish-brown crossbands. The adults are more nearly solid brown, with the bands mostly faded and confined to the lower sides of the body. When cornered, moccasins throw open their jaws, sheathed fangs projecting forward, to reveal a conspicuous white mouth lining, the source of their name. Peterson's *A Field Guide to Reptiles and Amphibians of Eastern and Central North America*, written by the herpetologist Roger Conant, warns, "Don't ever handle a live one!" I did so all the time, with the fifteen-year-old's naive confidence that I would never make a mistake.

Immature cottonmouths were never a problem, but one day I met an outsized adult that might easily have killed me. As I waded down one of the hatchery outflow streams, a very large snake crashed through the vegetation close to my legs and plunged into the water. I was especially startled by the movement because I had grown accustomed through the day to modestly proportioned frogs, snakes, and turtles quietly tensed on mudbanks and logs. This snake was more nearly my size as well as violent and noisy—a colleague, so to speak. It sped with wide body undulations to the center of the shallow watercourse and came to rest on a sandy riffle. It was the largest snake I had ever seen in the wild, more than five feet long with a body as thick as my arm and a head the size of my fist, only a bit under the published size record for the species. I was thrilled at the sight, and the snake looked as though it could be captured. It now lay quietly in the shallow clear water completely open to view, its body stretched along the fringing weeds, its head pointed back at an oblique angle to watch my approach. Cottonmouths are like that, even the young ones. They don't always undulate away until they are out of sight, in the manner of ordinary watersnakes. Although no emotion can be read in the frozen half-smile and staring yellow eyes, their reactions and postures give them an insolent air, as if they see their power reflected in the caution of human beings and other sizable enemies.

I moved into the snake handler's routine: pinned the body back of the head, grasped the neck behind the swelling masseteric muscles, and lifted the snake clear of the water. The big cottonmouth, so calm to that moment, reacted with stunning violence. Throwing its heavy body into convulsions, it twisted its head and neck slightly forward through my tightened fingers and stretched its mouth wide open to unfold inch-long fangs. A fetid musk from its anal glands filled the air. In the few seconds we were locked together the morning heat became more noticeable, reality crashed through, and at last I awoke from my dream and wondered why I was in that place alone. If I were bitten, who would find me? The snake began to turn its head far enough to clamp its jaws on my hand. I was not strong even for a boy of my slight size, and I was losing control. Reacting as by reflex, I heaved the giant out into the brush, and it thrashed frantically away, this time until it was out of sight and we were rid of each other.

This narrow escape was the most adrenaline-charged moment of my year's adventures at the hatchery. Since then I have cast back, trying to retrieve my emotions to understand why I explored swamps and hunted snakes with such dedication and recklessness. The activities gave me little or no heightened status among my peers; I never told anyone most of what I did. Pearl and my father were tolerant but not especially interested or encouraging; in any case I didn't say much to them either, for fear they would make me stay closer to home. My reasons were mixed. They were partly exhilaration at my entry into a beautiful and complex new world. And partly possessiveness; I had a place that no one else knew. And vanity; I believed that no one, anywhere, was better at exploring woods and finding snakes. And ambition; I dreamed I was training myself someday to be a professional field biologist. And finally, an undeciphered residue, a yearning remaining deep within me that I have never understood, nor wish to, for fear that if named it might vanish.

**Edward O. Wilson** *grew up in the South, spending most of his childhood in Alabama. He attended the University of Alabama, earned a Ph.D. from Harvard University, and went on to become one of the foremost natural scientists of his time. He recently retired from teaching at Harvard University and is the author of several books, including* Biophilia, Conciliation, *and his memoir,* Naturalist, *from which this excerpt is drawn.*

# Appendixes

# Ecology of the Gulf Coast

# What Is an Ecoregion?

The *Stories from Where We Live* series celebrates the literature of North America's diverse ecoregions. Ecoregions are large geographic areas that share similar climate, soils, and plant and animal communities. Thinking ecoregionally helps us understand how neighboring cities and states are connected, and makes it easier to coordinate the use and protection of shared rivers, forests, watersheds, mountain ranges, and other natural areas. We believe that ecoregions also provide an illuminating way to organize and compare place-based literature.

While many institutions have mapped the world's ecoregions, no existing delineation of ecoregions (or similar unit, such as *provinces* or *bioregions*) proved perfectly suited to a literary series. We created our own set of ecoregions based largely on existing scientific designations, with an added consideration for regional differences in human culture.

THE
NORTHWEST
PACIFIC
COAST
BOREAL
ROCKY MOUNTAINS
GREAT
NORTH
CALIFORNIA
COAST
WESTERN
DESERTS
AND
PLATEAUS
HAWAIIAN
ISLANDS

ARCTIC
FOREST
AMERICAN
PRAIRIE
GREAT LAKES
NORTHEAST WOODLANDS
NORTH ATLANTIC COAST
APPALACHIAN HIGHLANDS
SOUTH ATLANTIC COAST AND PIEDMONT
SOUTHERN HILL COUNTRY
GULF COAST

# Defining the Gulf Coast

The Gulf Coast ecoregion is an enormous horseshoe of land that encloses the warm waters of the Gulf of Mexico. It extends from eastern Mexico and Texas to Louisiana, Mississippi, and southern Alabama, to western and southernmost Florida. As horseshoes go, this one is a little warped. Its northern arc is distinctly thicker than its western and eastern sides. That's because the boundaries of the ecoregion coincide with the Gulf Coastal Plain—a broad, low-lying land area that reaches for some distance into inland parts of all these states but extends up the Mississippi Valley for several hundred miles.

Look at a map of the southern United States and you'll see that the Gulf of Mexico is almost an inland sea. It connects to the neighboring Caribbean Sea and Atlantic Ocean through two relatively narrow channels. The Yucatán Channel, located between Mexico's Yucatán Peninsula and western Cuba, lets in water from the Caribbean Sea. The water circulates clockwise, then exits out the Straits of Florida, which lie between Cuba and the Florida Keys. Because the water entering from the Caribbean is invariably quite warm, surface temperatures in the Gulf of Mexico hover around 70–80 degrees Fahrenheit. And this in turn creates the warm and humid breezes that inundate Gulf Coast communities for much of the year.

Despite the dominating presence of the Gulf of Mexico, one could argue that the region's rivers do as much or more to define the ecoregion. More than a dozen major rivers wind down through the region and empty out into the Gulf. To understand their influence, bear in mind that the topography of the Gulf Coast region is generally very flat—especially near the coast. In fact, the city of New Orleans actually lies below sea level! For this reason, large portions of the region experience regular flooding. In fact, many of the characteristic features of the Gulf Coast region—its bayous, its gumbo mud, its swamps, and even its mosquitoes—are a direct function of its low elevation and abundant water sources.

From a biological standpoint, the Gulf Coast region is marvelously rich. Warm temperatures and nutrient-rich waters encourage a profusion of plants, which in turn feed an array of marine and terrestrial animals. The Gulf of Mexico is one of our most important sources of shrimp and other seafood. Its coast provides a critical nesting ground for sea turtles and a welcome rest stop for migrating birds and butterflies. Overall it supports a staggering diversity of wildlife species, from tiny pygmy blue butterflies to thousand-pound manatees!

But there's another side to this biological diversity. Swarms of mosquitoes, several varieties of poisonous snakes, stinging rays, and scratching nettles have long given the Gulf Coast region the reputation of being a bit inhospitable to humans. Much of the work of eighteenth, nineteenth, and early twentieth century settlers was to subdue these offending elements. Attitudes have changed, however, and many Gulf Coast residents are now actively involved in protecting the region's rich natural resources. Still, one can't help but marvel at the sense of humor, present in so much of Gulf Coast writing, that has flourished under these often challenging conditions.

Culturally speaking, the Gulf Coast is very diverse. First inhabited by Choctaw, Pascagoula, and other Indian groups, it was later heavily traveled by French and Spanish explorers. The establishment of cotton and sugar plantations led to the brutal importation of Africans and African Americans from other parts of the South to work the fields as slaves. Unrest in Canada prompted the settlement of many Acadian, or Cajun, communities. Immigrants from Mexico, Cuba, and other parts of Latin America settled large portions of the region, especially in Texas and Florida. Descendants of all these groups and more still live along the Gulf Coast, giving rise to a tremendous variety of artistic and musical traditions, dialects, foods, and holidays, as well as stories that tell of their forebears' experiences, and their own, in this life-filled region.

# Habitats

If you were to walk along the edge of the Gulf of Mexico, you'd cover more than 3,600 miles of coastline in the United States portion alone. In the process, you'd pass through dozens of different *habitats*—areas that provide animals with the particular food and environmental conditions they need to survive. The habitats of the Gulf Coast include coral reefs, freshwater and saltwater marshes, gum ponds, wet prairies, tropical hardwood hammocks, floodplain forests, and pine flatwoods. We've described some of the most prominent of these habitats in the section below.

*Beaches and Dunes:* The sandy beach habitat that many humans find so restful is actually a very restless environment. Pounding waves, strong, salty winds, and sparse vegetation combine to make beaches and dunes inhospitable to most animals. Clams and sea worms survive by burrowing under the sand and staying moist, waiting for the surf to serve up a fresh wallop of food-filled water. Plovers, oystercatchers, and other shorebirds scout for small sea creatures marooned by the ebbing tide. Farther up the beach, sea oats anchor themselves in the sand with a dense network of roots, stabilizing the sand enough to form dunes. Behind these dunes grow thickets of wax myrtle, saw palmetto, other hardy trees, and even whole maritime forests.

Sandy beaches are the dominant shoreline habitat in many parts of the Gulf Coast ecoregion. They also cover parts of the many barrier islands that lie parallel to the shore. In southern Texas and southwestern Florida, shallow and gentle waters create ideal breeding grounds for mollusks and make the beaches splendid places to search for intact seashells. (Examples: "Port O'Connor 9/1/99"; "Buried Christmas Tree"; "Eulogy for a Hermit Crab.")

***Sea-Grass Beds:*** Dive into the waters along much of the northeast Gulf of Mexico and you may find yourself skimming across underwater meadows of shoal grass, turtle grass, and widgeon grass. These sea-grass beds form at depths of up to seventy feet, but are often found in shallow water. Studded with tiny marine animals and surrounded by numerous species of algae, the swaying grasses attract fish, crabs, shrimp, and snails. Manatees paddle by to munch on underwater plants. And snorkelers stop by in search of scallops. (Example: "Scalloping.")

***Salt Marshes and Estuaries:*** Salt marshes lie on the ocean's edge, often at the meeting place of freshwater and salt water. You can recognize them by densely growing black needlerush, salt meadow cordgrass, and smooth cordgrass, and by water depths that shift depending on the tides. They often surround estuaries–rich brackish waters that form where rivers empty out into the sea.

Salt marshes aren't known for having a great diversity of plant species. Instead, their claim to fame is exceptional productivity. Nourished by regular tides and sustained by rapid rates of decay, salt marshes are chock-full of nutrients. That's one reason both salt marshes and estuaries serve as nurseries for baby fish, young shellfish, and ducklings. In addition, salt marshes attract scores of wading birds that hide among the tall grasses and gobble up stranded fish. Introduced nutria flourish in the matted grasses that cover the salt marsh bottom. (Example: "Rockefeller Wildlife Preserve: Mid-August.")

***Mangrove Forests:*** If you were to try to walk the perimeter of Florida's peninsula, you'd find tough going in the densely grown mangrove forests that line much of the central and southern coasts. The word "mangrove" refers to a group of tropical trees that have some remarkable adaptations to their waterlogged coastal home. In Florida, red mangroves grow closest to the water, gaining support and oxygen through exposed roots, called "prop roots," that arch away from their trunks. Black mangroves, which grow behind red mangroves, breathe through a bunch of fingerlike branches that grow up out of their roots. White mangroves grow still farther back from the shore, increasing their oxygen intake through tiny root hairs under the soil's surface.

Mangroves produce seeds that start growing into young plants while they are still attached to the parent tree. When they finally fall, these seeds can float in the water for great distances until they reach an exposed bank of soil. Red mangroves can colonize the slightest bit of exposed beach, eventually making it stable enough for other species.

Florida's mangrove forests are among the most extensive in the world. Here you'll find all sorts of insects, fish, and invertebrates living in the pools of water between the mangrove roots. Great flocks of waterbirds roost in the trees—including magnificent frigate birds, roseate

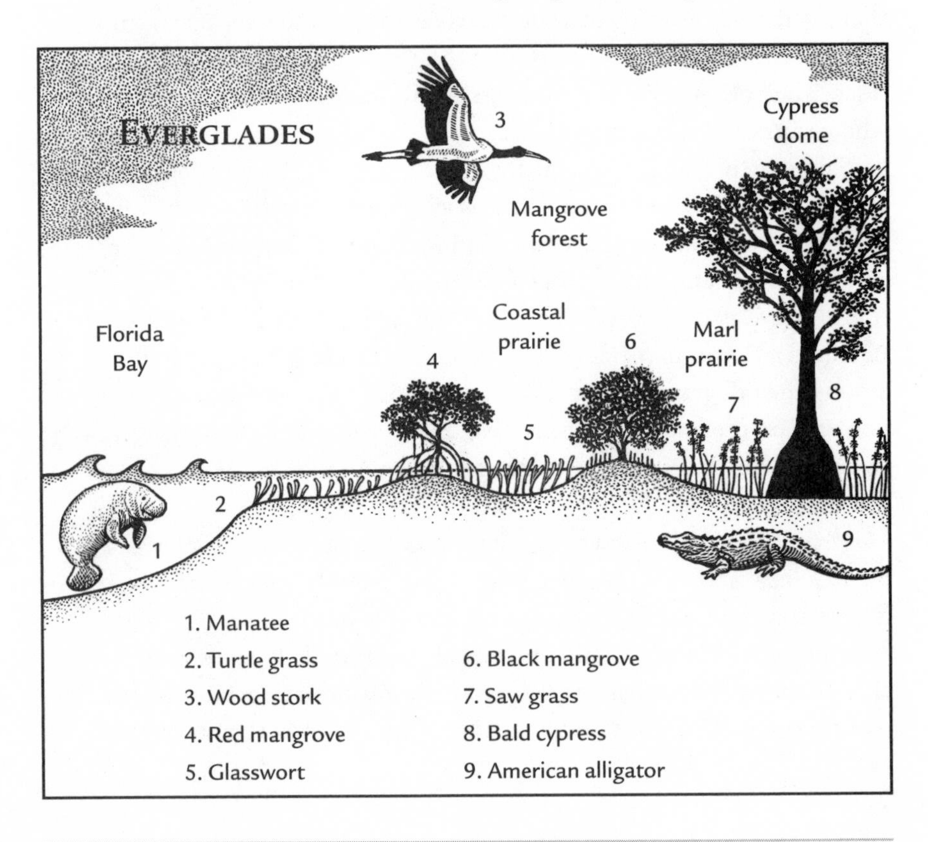

spoonbills, wood storks, pelicans, white ibises, herons, and egrets. You might spot a black-whiskered vireo flitting in the canopy or a mangrove salt marsh snake hanging from a low branch. But you'll really have to keep your eyes peeled to see the reclusive mangrove cuckoos hiding in the trees. (Example: "Kenzie's Plunge into Paradise.")

***The Everglades:*** Imagine a river sixty miles wide and rarely more than knee-deep. Imagine it flowing southward for three hundred miles, so slowly that you can't even detect a current. Imagine it wending its way through acres of saw grass, surrounding tiny wooded islands, and tickling the roots of mangrove trees as it empties into the sea. Imagine all this—and a colorful community of crocodiles, manatees, ibises, tree snails, and more—and you have a pretty good picture of the Florida Everglades.

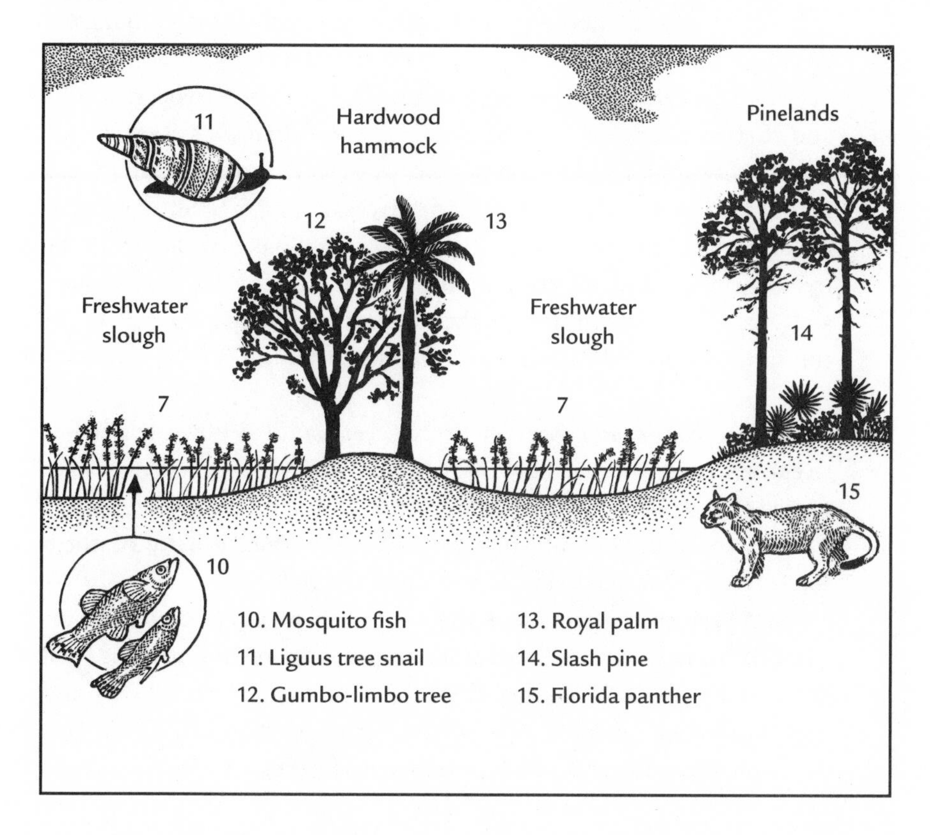

The Everglades is unlike any other river on Earth, and it's the only flooded grassland in North America. Human activities—farming, home building, and, above all, water diversion—have radically altered this river of grass and reduced it to less than half of its original size. But it still supports a stunning variety of species. Florida panthers prowl through the scrub in search of deer, rabbits, and other prey. Snail kites fly in a low patrol, on the lookout for apple snails. And alligators dig out watering holes in times of drought that may end up supporting everything from schools of fish to thirsty deer and raccoons. (Examples: "The Flood"; "The Lure of the Swamp"; "Alligator Crossing.")

*Freshwater Swamps:* Although the term "swamp" is probably misapplied to a variety of wetlands, few habitats are more widespread and characteristic of the Gulf Coast region. Usually lining rivers or lakes, swamps experience regular flooding and have a distinctly soggy character. Cypress swamps are filled with tall bald cypresses or shorter pond cypresses. You can readily recognize these trees by their swollen trunks and their roots, which sometimes form cone-shaped "knees." Other common swamp trees include water tupelo, black gum, and red maple. Plant life in these habitats is lush, with trees draped in Spanish moss or in some places covered with orchids and ferns. Snakes slither from the trees to the ground, alligators loiter beneath the surface of the water, and swamp sparrows sing from their treetop perch. (Examples: "Lost in the Swamp"; "Into the Bayous"; "Alabama Dreaming.")

*Bottomland Hardwood Forests:* If you've ever paddled down the major rivers and streams that flow into the Gulf of Mexico, you may have passed through the region's leafy green bottomland hardwood forests. Thanks to abundant moisture and sunlight, the diversity of these forests rivals that of coral reefs and tropical rain forests.

Each year, spring rains soak the watershed, picking up dirt and organic debris as they drain into local waterways. Rivers and streams swell and pick up speed. When they flood their banks their speed slows, and they drop their nutrient-rich silt onto the surrounding land. This yearly nutrient dump supplies bottomland forests with fertile soils. In addition, heavy moisture increases rates of decay, recycling nutrients quickly back into the system. Add to this the high temperatures and abundant sunlight of the region, and the result is high productivity: towering hickories, soaring sycamores, and single water oak trees producing nearly 30,000 acorns in one year! Not surprisingly, these forests are bursting with wildlife, from barred owls to mud snakes to swamp rabbits to tree frogs. (Examples: "My First Dog"; "The Alligator and the Hunter"; "The Ivory-Billed Woodpecker.")

***Lakes and Rivers:*** The Mississippi. The Choctahatchee. The Atchafalaya and the Apalachicola. The Gulf Coast ecoregion is blessed with an abundance of rivers and streams, many of which bear their original Indian names. But look at a map and you'll notice relatively few large lakes dotting the region. That's because most of North America's lakes were carved into the earth by advancing glaciers, and these glaciers never reached the southern part of the continent. As a result, most of the region's lakes are human-made reservoirs.

Still, there is no absence of magnificent freshwater habitat in the Gulf Coast region. A number of slow, muddy, nutrient-rich rivers meander south to the Gulf and nourish the swamps and floodplain forests on either side of their shores. The Mississippi is one of the largest such rivers in the country. Smaller slow-moving rivers are called bayous. Fish, frogs, turtles, and ducks all gather in the rivers and bayous of the Gulf Coast. Herons, kingfishers, and a multitude of other birds flock to their shores. (Examples: "The Singing River"; "Mollie Tree.")

***Pine Forests:*** Pine trees are the pioneers of the tree world. Their light seeds spread easily into recently cleared sites. They germinate, sprout, and grow to great heights when bathed in bright sunlight. But in most cases, once pine trees have grown tall enough to block sunlight from the forest floor, their seedlings can't compete with those of shade-loving hardwoods. For this reason, and if regular fires don't restart the process, pine forests generally give way to hardwoods.

Magnificent forests of longleaf pines once flourished across much of the southern United States, sustained by natural fires or those started by American Indians. Fires also cleared out the undergrowth; only a carpet of wire grass or saw palmetto covered the ground. You can still find forests of slash pine, loblolly pine, and even longleaf pine in some parts of the Gulf Coast region these days, although they've been much reduced by logging, agriculture, fire suppression, pine plantations, and urban development. Where they grow, you may find armadillos snatching up insects, woodpeckers hopping down tree trunks, and gopher tortoises sharing their thirty-foot burrows with rabbits, raccoons, skinks, lizards, and toads. One creature that has come to symbolize the importance of wild, old-growth pine forests is the red-cockaded woodpecker. These rare woodpeckers require old trees with rotted centers to use as nests. Red-cockaded woodpeckers tear open tree bark to get at the insects inside, much like a partygoer bursts a piñata. Once the damage is done, pine warblers, nuthatches, Carolina chickadees, and tufted titmice race in to snatch up their share of the feast! (Example: "Where the Wild Animals Is Plentiful.")

***Farms, Gardens, and Backyards:*** If you were to fly over the Gulf Coast region, the largest open expanses you'd see, besides the Gulf itself, would be vast acres of farmland. Many of these farms are located on the southern "Black Belt"—a band of exceptionally fertile soil that crosses parts of Louisiana, Mississippi, and Alabama. These soils once supported millions of acres of grasslands and, with them, many plants and animals. But even today's open farmland provides living space for a number of wildife species. Crows snatch meals from the growing crops, and hawks hunt for rodents on the exposed hills. Wildflowers spring up in unmowed roadsides.

You can also find a surprising variety of life in the vacant lots, gardens, and backyards of the more urbanized sections of the Gulf Coast. Songbirds, bees, butterflies, and small mammals can all survive in these small green spaces, especially if they're supported by native plantings. (Examples: "Vacant Lot"; "Remembering Bull Run Road"; "Jewels of the Night"; "Crows in the Yard.")

# Animals and Plants

The Gulf Coast ecoregion is home to a tremendous variety of plants and animals. We've listed below only those wild species that are mentioned in the anthology.

*Birds:* Scientists and bird-watchers sometimes group birds into simple categories as a way to help organize and identify them. *Swimmers* of the Gulf Coast include anhingas (sometimes called snakebirds), Canada geese, gallinules, coots, and cormorants. *Aerialists,* or flyers, include laughing gulls, terns, and white and brown pelicans. A large number of *long-legged wading birds* fill the wetlands of the region, including great blue herons, great white herons, wood storks, roseate spoonbills, snowy egrets, and whooping cranes. Bobwhites and wild turkeys are *fowl-like birds*. Osprey, peregrine falcons, vultures (sometimes called buzzards), and owls are *birds of prey*. Crows, mockingbirds, purple martins, and blue jays are among the region's *perching birds*. *Nonperching land birds* of the past and present include ivory-billed woodpeckers and other woodpeckers, and doves.

Purple Gallinule

Roseate Spoonbill

*Mammals:* Wild mammals inhabiting the Gulf Coast region include squirrels, marsh rabbits and other rabbits, armadillos, opossum, raccoons, skunks, fox, northern river otters, razorback hogs, javelinas, black bears, coyotes, white-tailed deer, Key deer, bobcats (which May Jordan sometimes called wildcats or lynx), mink (which May Jordan

Swamp Rabbit

sometimes called pine martens), weasels, and Florida panthers. Marine mammals include dolphins and manatees. Red wolves, nearly hunted to extinction, have been reintroduced to pockets of Louisiana. The "wildcat civet" mentioned in the journals of May Jordan probably was an eastern spotted skunk. Her report of a badger was undoubtedly an error.

Florida Panther

*Marine Invertebrates:* Many *mollusks* dwell in the Gulf of Mexico, including squid, oysters, scallops, conchs, and lightning whelks. Jellyfish are *jellylike animals. Arthropods* include shrimp, barnacles, blue crabs, ghost crabs, and horseshoe crabs. The spiny-skinned *echinoderms* include sea stars (or starfish), sea urchins, and sand dollars.

Ghost Crab

*Freshwater and Terrestrial Invertebrates:* Crayfish (also called crawdads) are *freshwater invertebrates. Terrestrial invertebrates* (those that live on land) include spiders and centipedes and a great number of insects, including bees, ants, monarch butterflies and other butterflies, mosquitoes, cicadas, weevils, crickets, stinkbugs, dragonflies, and fireflies.

Red Ant

*Reptiles and Amphibians:* Softshelled turtles and other turtles are among the many *reptiles* of the Gulf Coast region, as are a wealth of snakes, including flat-tailed water snakes, diamondback rattlesnakes, eastern ribbon snakes, green water snakes, mud snakes, and cottonmouth moccasins. Alligators and crocodiles are the largest reptiles of the region. Although alligators are widely distributed throughout the Gulf Coast, crocodiles reside only in parts of southern Florida. One way to distinguish between the two species is by comparing their "smiles." When their mouths are closed, only

Cottonmouth Water Moccasin

American Alligator

crocodiles boast a set of protruding bottom teeth. Among the many *amphibians* that occupy this region are amphiuma and other salamanders, and frogs.

***Fish:*** *Saltwater bony fish* of the Gulf Coast region include mackerel, flounder, redfish, toadfish (or mudfish), and croakers. *Freshwater bony fish* include gar, bluegill (breams), perch, bigmouth buffalo (buffalo fish), trout, and catfish. Nurse sharks and other sharks, skates, and stingrays (sometimes called stingarees) are all in a special group of fish known as *cartilaginous fish.*

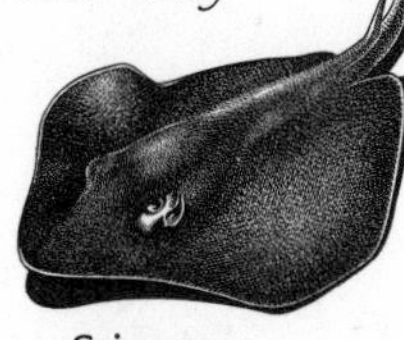
Stingray

***Plants:*** Tall, broadleaf trees include live oaks, blackjack oaks, flowering dogwood, black tupelo (or black gum), magnolias, chinaberry, willows, coconut palm and other palms, sweet gum, pecan, common persimmon, fringe tree (which May Jordan called grandpa gray beard), and buttonwood and other kinds of mangroves. Coniferous trees include bald cypress, red cedars, and a variety of pines. Wax myrtle, saw palmetto, and marsh elder are described as smaller broadleaf shrubs. Generally speaking, the following are all wildflowers: salt marsh fleabane, clover, muscadine grape, phragmites (also called Roseau cane), swamp lily, water lilies, water lettuce, cordgrass, needlerush (or needle grass), Saint Augustine grass, cabomba, catbrier, yellow jessamine, common milkweed, peppergrass, saw grass, sedges, sorrels, poke sallet, wild onions, wild garlic, southern dewberries, and blackberries. Johnson grass and cuckleburrows are invasive weeds. Spanish moss and other bromeliads are known as *epiphytes,* or air plants, because they live entirely on a host tree.

Cabbage Palmetto Tree

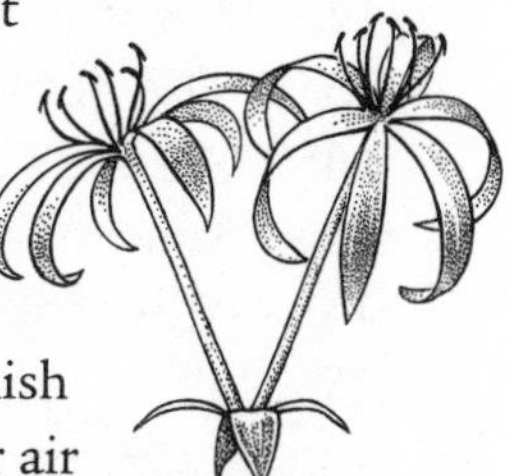
Swamp Lily

# Stories by State

### Alabama

1. "Southern Winter" (Tuscaloosa)
2. "Crazy" (Shorter)
3. "Where the Wild Animals Is Plentiful" (Washington County)
4. "Mollie Tree" (Geneva County)
5. "Fig Picking" (Bay Minette)
6. "The Ivory-Billed Woodpecker" *(also Louisiana and Mississippi)*
7. "Alabama Dreaming" (Brewton)

### Florida

8. "The Flood" (Belle Glade)
9. "Lost in the Swamp" (western Florida)
10. "Scalloping" (Port St. Joe)
11. "The Lure of the Swamp" (Corkscrew Swamp)
12. "Florida Haiku" (Cape Coral)
13. "The Season of Jellyfish" (Cudjoe Key)
14. "Kenzie's Plunge into Paradise" (Big Pine Key)
15. "Swimming with Mermaids" (Crystal River)
16. "Alligator Crossing" (Everglades National Park)
17. "The Dead Shark" (Anna Maria Island)
18. "Manatee" (Fort Myers)

### Louisiana

19. "The Midnight Marsh" (Alligator Bayou)

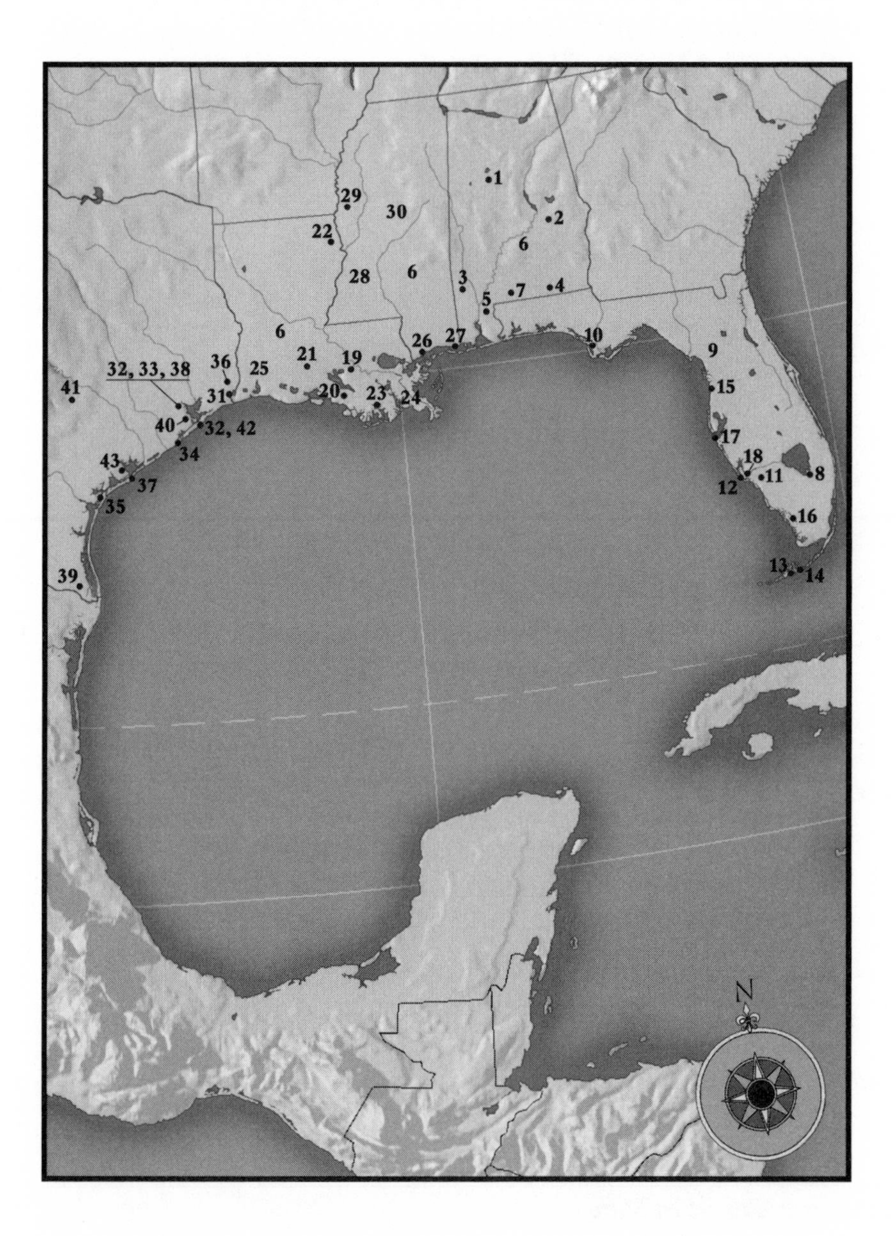
1
29
30
2
22
6
28
6
3
7
4
5
6
26
27
10
9
32, 33, 38
36
25
21
19
41
31
20
23
24
15
40
32, 42
34
17
43
37
18
11
8
12
35
16
39
13
14
N

20. "Into the Bayous" (Atchafalaya Basin)
21. "Rockefeller Wildlife Preserve: Mid-August"
22. "Remembering Bull Run Road" (Melbourne Community)
23. "Cleaning Redfish with Uncle" (Houma)
24. "Public School" (southeastern Louisiana)
25. "Why Alligator Hates Dog"
6. "The Ivory-Billed Woodpecker" *(also Alabama and Mississippi)*

Mississippi

26. "A Creature in the Bay of St. Louis" (Bay St. Louis)
27. "The Singing River" (Pascagoula)
28. "The Alligator and the Hunter"
29. "The Soul of Southern Cooking" (Hollandale)
30. "Mosquito Blues"
6. "The Ivory-Billed Woodpecker" *(also Alabama and Louisiana)*

Texas

31. "Vacant Lot" (Port Arthur)
32. "Searching for Ed Palmer" (Houston and Galveston)
33. "Still Weather" (Houston)
34. "Buried Christmas Tree" (Surfside)
35. "Winter Texans in Aransas" (Aransas National Wildlife Refuge)
36. "My First Dog" (Neches River Bottom)
37. "Port O'Connor 9/1/99" (Port O'Connor)
38. "Jewels of the Night" (Houston)
39. "My Mother Returns to Calaboz" (El Calaboz)
40. "Crows in the Yard" (Friendswood)
41. "The Softshell Turtle" (San Marcos)
42. "Eulogy for a Hermit Crab" (Galveston)
43. "Migration Midpoint: What We Can See from Here" (Port Lavaca)

# Parks and Preserves

Listed below are just a few of the many places where you can go to experience the wilder side of the Gulf Coast ecoregion. Bear in mind that some of these states straddle more than one ecoregion; we have included only natural areas in the Gulf Coast portion of the states. Also, please note that the phone numbers provided sometimes are for the park's headquarters, but often are for a managing agency or organization. In any case, the people at these numbers can provide you with details about the area and directions for how to get there.

## Alabama

Choctaw National Wildlife Refuge (Butler) 334-246-3583
Conecuh National Forest (Andalusia) 334-222-2555
Dauphin Island Bird Sanctuary (Dauphin Island) 334-861-3607
Fort Toulouse State Monument (Wetumpka) 334-567-3002
Gulf State Park (Gulf Shores) 334-948-7275
Mobile-Tensaw Delta (Spanish Fort) 334-626-5474
Moundville Archaeological Park (Moundville) 205-371-2524
Oak Mountain State Park (Pelham) 205-620-2524
Talladega National Forest (Oakmulgee Ranger District) 256-463-2273
Wheeler National Wildlife Refuge (Decatur) 256-350-6639

## Florida

Apalachicola National Forest (Bristol) 850-643-2282 (west) or 850-926-3561 (east)
Blackwater River State Park (Munson) 850-983-5363
Cedar Key National Wildlife Refuge (Cedar Key) 352-493-0238
Corkscrew Swamp Sanctuary (Sebastian) 941-348-9151

Edward Ball Wakulla Springs State Park (Wakulla Springs) 850-922-3632
Everglades National Park (Homestead) 305-242-7700
Fakahatchee Strand Preserve State Park (Copeland) 239-695-4593
Florida Caverns State Park (Marianna) 850-482-9598
Fort De Soto Park (Tierra Verde) 727-582-2267
Honeymoon Island State Recreation Area (Dunedin) 727-469-5942
J. N. "Ding" Darling National Wildlife Refuge (Sanibel) 941-472-1100
Lower Suwanee National Wildlife Refuge (Chiefland) 352-493-0238
Manatee Springs State Park (Chiefland) 352-493-6072
Myakka River State Park (Sarasota) 941-361-6511
National Key Deer Refuge (Big Pine Key) 305-872-0774
Oscar Scherer State Park (Osprey) 941-483-5956
St. Andrews State Park (Panama City Beach) 850-233-5140
St. Joseph Peninsula State Park (St. Joseph Peninsula) 850-227-1327
St. Mark's National Wildlife Refuge (St. Mark's) 850-925-6121
Suwanee River State Park (Live Oak) 386-362-2746
Torreya State Park (Bristol) 850-643-2674

### Louisiana

Atchafalaya Basin (Henderson) 318-291-8448
Audubon Louisiana Nature Center (New Orleans) 504-246-5672
Audubon Park and Zoological Garden (New Orleans) 504-581-4629 or 800-774-7394
Audubon State Historic Site (St. Francisville) 225-635-3739
Avery Island/Jungle Gardens (Avery Island) 337-369-6243
Briarwood: Caroline Dormon Nature Preserve (Saline) 318-576-3379 (afternoons and evenings)
Cajun Prairie Preservation Project (Eunice) 337-550-1245
Catahoula National Wildlife Refuge (Jena) 318-992-5261
D'Arbonne National Wildlife Refuge (West Monroe) 318-726-4222
Honey Island Swamp (Slidell) 985-641-1769
Jean Lafitte National Historical Park and Preserve (Marrero) 504-589-2636 or 504-589-3882
Joyce Wildlife Management Area (Pontchatoula) 225-556-9890

Kisatchie National Forest (Pineville) 318-473-7160 or 318-352-2568
Lacassine National Wildlife Refuge (Lake Arthur) 337-774-5923
Peveto Woods Sanctuary (Cameron Parish) 225-757-1769
Rockefeller Refuge (Grand Chenier) 337-538-2276
Sabine National Wildlife Refuge (Hackberry) 337-762-3816
Tensas River National Wildlife Refuge (Tallulah) 318-574-2664

### Mississippi

Bienville National Forest (Forest) 601-469-3811
Crosby Arboretum (Picayune) 601-799-2311
De Soto National Forest (Hattiesburg) 601-928-5291
Delta National Forest (Rolling Fork) 662-873-6256
Gulf Islands National Seashore (Ocean Springs) 228-875-3962 or 228-875-9057
Holly Springs National Forest (Oxford) 662-236-6550
Homochitto National Forest (Meadville) 601-384-5876
J. P. Coleman State Park (Iuka) 662-423-6515
Least Tern Nesting Areas (Gulfport) 228-896-0055 or 228-864-1335
Mississippi Sandhill Crane National Wildlife Refuge (Gautier) 228-497-6322
Natchez Trace Parkway (Natchez) 800-657-3775
Noxubee National Wildlife Refuge (Starkville) 662-323-5548
Panther Swamp National Wildlife Refuge (Yazoo City) 662-746-5060
Plymouth Bluff Environmental Center (Columbus) 662-241-6214
Vicksburg National Military Park (Vicksburg) 601-636-0583
Yazoo National Wildlife Refuge (Hollandale) 662-839-2638

### Texas

Anahuac National Wildlife Refuge (Anahuac) 409-267-3337
Aransas and Amatagorda Island Wildlife Refuges (Austwell) 361-286-3559
Big Thicket National Preserve (Beaumont) 409-246-2337
Brazos Bend State Park (Needville) 979-553-5101
Galveston Island State Park (Galveston) 409-737-1222
Goose Island State Park (Rockport) 361-729-2858

Lake Houston State Park (New Caney) 281-354-6881
Matagorda Island State Park (Port O'Connor) 361-983-2215
McFaddin-Texas Point National Wildlife Refuge (Sabine Pass) 409-971-2909
Mustang Island State Park (Port Aransas) 361-749-5246
Padre Island National Seashore (Corpus Christi) 361-949-8068
San Bernard National Wildlife Refuge (Brazoria) 409-849-6062
Sea Rim State Park (Sabine Pass) 409-971-2559
Sheldon Lake State Park (Houston) 281-456-2800

# Recommended Reading

Alden, Peter, et al. *National Audubon Society Field Guide to Florida.* New York: Alfred A. Knopf, 1998.

Alden, Peter, et al. *National Audubon Society Field Guide to the Southeastern States.* New York: Alfred A. Knopf, 1999.

Amos, William, and Stephen H. Amos. *Atlantic and Gulf Coasts* (Audubon Society Nature Guides). New York: Alfred A. Knopf, 1985.

Blaustein, Daniel. *The Everglades and the Gulf Coast* (Ecosystems of America Series, Set 2). Tarrytown, N.Y.: Benchmark Books, 2000.

Douglas, Marjory Stoneman. *The Everglades: River of Grass.* New York: Rinehart, 1947, and Sarasota: Pineapple Press, 1997.

*Gulf Coast Seashore Life* (Pocket Naturalist Series). Blaine, Wash.: Waterford Press, 1997.

Hansen, Gunnar. *Islands at the Edge of Time: A Journey to America's Barrier Islands.* Washington, D.C.: Island Press, 1993.

Jenkins, Peter. *Along the Edge of America.* Boston, Mass.: Houghton Mifflin, 1997.

Miller, Brian K., and William R. Fontenot. *Birds of the Gulf Coast.* Baton Rouge: Louisiana State University Press, 2001.

# Special Thanks

Working on an anthology of the Gulf Coast in the middle of one of Massachusetts's longest and snowiest winters was in some ways consoling and in other ways a challenge. I'm grateful for the assistance of many friends, colleagues, librarians, and gracious and informative Gulf Coast residents.

Many thanks to Eric Rosenberg, Priscilla Howell, and Joe Taylor, who connected me with writing from the Gulf Coast region that I might not otherwise have found.

Miriam Stewart, Jen Lindstrom, Priscilla Howell, and Robin Kelsey read submissions and draft manuscripts. I thoroughly enjoyed our accompanying conversations, when we stayed on topic and when we didn't.

Widener Library, ever surprising me with the breadth and depth of its resources, supplied more than a few wonderful Gulf Coast selections. The Julia Child cookbook collection at Radcliffe's Schlesinger Library thrilled me by having *The Soul of Southern Cooking* on its shelves. And the librarians at Cambridge Public Library, who could moonlight as private eyes, traced an out-of-print novel to a public library in Bangor, Maine, and brought it back to me through interlibrary loan. Even my abundant library fines cannot begin to repay them for their services.

I also took advantage of the fascinating collection of historical and contemporary books on natural history at Harvard's Museum of Comparative Zoology Library. With these resources I was able to determine such things as the historical range of badgers, the southern equivalent of a pine marten, and the scientific names for buffalo fish and mud fish.

A few experts in southern history and ecology reviewed my manuscript for errors and oversights. Heartfelt thanks go to Lisa Lindquist Dorr, assistant professor of history at the University of Alabama, to Jenny Cook, marine educator at Dauphin Island Sea Lab, and to Alan Scott of Everglades National Park for their insightful comments.

Every anthology in this series has been shaped by the multitude of writers whose works grace its pages. The writers I worked with on this anthology were an exceptionally dedicated and diligent bunch, taking the time not only to tighten their own pieces but also to enrich my understanding of their region. My thanks go out to them, and to all who honor a region through written and spoken words.

# Contributor Acknowledgments

Kelly King Alexander, "The Midnight Marsh," *Cricket* 24, no. 9 (May 1997): 44. Copyright © 1997 by Kelly King Alexander. Reprinted with permission from *Cricket* magazine.

John James Audubon, "The Ivory-Billed Woodpecker," excerpted from *Ornithological Biography* (Edinburgh: A. Black, 1839). Also in *John James Audubon: Writings and Drawings,* ed. Christopher Irmscher (New York: Library of America, 1999), 270–75.

Jill Barrie, "Manatee," *The Ledge* 7, no. 24 (Fall/Winter 2000): 75. Copyright © 2000 by Jill Barrie. Reprinted with permission from the author.

Jack B. Bedell, "Cleaning Redfish with Uncle," in *At the Bonehouse* (Huntsville: Texas Review Press, 1998), 40. Copyright © 1998 by Jack B. Bedell. Reprinted with permission from the author.

Charles Bergman, "Swimming with Mermaids," *Orion* 10 (Summer 1991): 18–27. Also in *Finding Home,* ed. Peter Sauer (Boston: Beacon Press, 1992), 278–80, 287–88. Copyright © 1991 by Charles Bergman. Reprinted with permission from the author.

Joseph Bruchac, "The Alligator and the Hunter," in *Native American Animal Stories* (Golden, Colo.: Fulcrum Publishing, 1992), 91–95. Copyright © 1992 by Joseph Bruchac. Reprinted with permission from Fulcrum Publishing, Inc., Golden, Colorado. All rights reserved.

SuzAnne C. Cole, "Jewels of the Night." Copyright © 2002 by SuzAnne C. Cole. Printed with permission from the author.

John Cutrone, "The Lure of the Swamp." Copyright © 2002 by John Cutrone. Printed with permission from the author.

Reese Danley-Kilgo, "Mollie Tree," in *Gifts from Our Grandmothers,* ed. Carol Dovi (New York: Crown Publishers, 2000), 184. Copyright © 2000 by Reese Danley-Kilgo. Reprinted with permission from the author.

Bonnie J. Doerr, "Kenzie's Plunge into Paradise." Copyright © 2002 by Bonnie J. Doerr. Printed with permission from the author.

Marjory Stoneman Douglas, "Alligator Crossing," excerpted from *Alligator Crossing* (New York: John Day Company, 1959), 120–23. Copyright © 1959 by Marjory Stoneman Douglas. Reprinted with permission from the University of Miami. *A new edition of* Alligator Crossing *will be published by Milkweed Editions in the spring of 2003.*

Stuart Dybek, "The Season of Jellyfish," *Chowder Review* 5 (Fall 1975). Copyright © 1975 by Stuart Dybek. Reprinted with permission from the author.

I. C. Eason, "My First Dog," in *The Stories of I. C. Eason,* as told to Blair Pittman (Denton: University of North Texas Press, 1996), 6–13. Copyright © 1996 by Blair Pittman. Reprinted with permission from University of North Texas Press.

Andreanna Edwards, "Scalloping." Copyright © 2002 by Andreanna Edwards. Printed with permission from the author.

Barry Hannah, "A Creature in the Bay of St. Louis," in *High Lonesome* (New York: Atlantic Monthly Press, 1996), 45–51. Copyright © 1996 by Barry Hannah. Reprinted with permission from Grove/Atlantic, Inc. and the author.

Ziporah Hildebrandt, "The Dead Shark." Copyright © 2002 by Ziporah Hildebrandt. Printed with permission from the author.

Zora Neale Hurston, "The Flood," excerpted from *Their Eyes Were Watching God* (New York: Perennial Library, 1990), 146–58. Copyright © 1937 by Harper and Row, Publishers. Renewed 1965 by John C. Hurston and Joel Hurston. Reprinted with permission from HarperCollins Publishers, Inc.

Angela Johnson, "Crazy," in *The Other Side: Shorter Poems* (New York: Orchard Books, 1998), 26–27. Copyright © 1998 by Angela Johnson. Reprinted with permission from Orchard Books, an imprint of Scholastic Inc.

May Jordan, "Where the Wild Animals Is Plentiful," excerpted from *Where the Wild Animals Is Plentiful,* ed. Elisa Moore Baldwin (Tuscaloosa: University of Alabama Press, 1999), 35–37, 39, 41, 43, 46–48, 50–51, 55–56, 59–62, 80, 82–83. Copyright © 1999 by University of Alabama Press. Reprinted with permission from University of Alabama Press.

Rob Kerr, "Searching for Ed Palmer." Copyright © 2002 by Rob Kerr. Printed with permission from the author.

Cassandra King, "Fig Picking," in *Belles' Letters: Contemporary Fiction by Alabama Women,* ed. Joe Taylor and Tina N. Jones (Livingston, Ala.: Livingston Press, 1999), 47–55. Copyright © 1999 by Cassandra King. Reprinted with permission from the author.

Norbert Krapf, "Into the Bayous," *Louisiana Review* 3, no. 1 (Summer 1974), 18. Copyright © 1974 by Norbert Krapf. Reprinted with permission from the author.

Mary Beth Lundgren, "Florida Haiku." Copyright © 2002 by Mary Beth Lundgren. Printed with permission from the author.

Kevin Maher, "Rockefeller Wildlife Preserve: Mid-August," in *River of Words,* selected by Robert Hass (Berkeley, Calif.: River of Words, 2000), 3–4. Copyright © 2000 by River of Words Project. Reprinted with permission from River of Words.

Katrinka Moore, "Crows in the Yard." Copyright © 2002 by Katrinka Moore. Printed with permission from the author.

John Muir, "Lost in the Swamp," excerpted from *A Thousand-Mile Walk to the Gulf* (Boston: Houghton Mifflin Company, 1916), 111–16, 118–21.

Carol Munn, "Still Weather." Copyright © 2002 by Carol Munn. Printed with permission from the author.

Christa Pandey, "Southern Winter." Copyright © 2002 by Christa Pandey. Printed with permission from the author.

Virginia E. Parker-Staat, "Winter Texans in Aransas." Copyright © 2002 by Virginia E. Parker-Staat. Printed with permission from the author.

J. J. Reneaux, "Why Alligator Hates Dog," in *Cajun Folktales* (Little Rock: August House Publishers, 1992), 17–20. Copyright © 1992 by J. J. Reneaux. Reprinted with permission from August House Publishers, Inc.

Pattiann Rogers, "Eulogy for a Hermit Crab," in *Song of the World Becoming: New and Collected Poems 1981–2001* (Minneapolis: Milkweed Editions, 2001), 189. Copyright © 1986 by Pattiann Rogers.

Dorothy Shawhan, "Mosquito Blues," *Delta Scene* 10 (Summer 1983), 7–9, 24–25, and reprinted in *A Place Called Mississippi,* ed. Marion Barnwell (Jackson: University Press of Mississippi, 1997), 134–40. Copyright © 1983 by Dorothy Shawhan. Reprinted with permission from the author.

Kathy Starr, "The Soul of Southern Cooking," excerpted from *The Soul of Southern Cooking* (Jackson: University Press of Mississippi, 1989), xvii–xx, 3, 53–54, 91–92, 137–39. Copyright © 1989 by University Press of Mississippi. Reprinted with permission from University Press of Mississippi.

Margo Tamez, "My Mother Returns to Calaboz." Copyright © 2002 by Margo Tamez. Printed with permission from the author.

Shellie Rushing Tomlinson, "Remembering Bull Run Road." Copyright © 2002 by Shellie Rushing Tomlinson. Printed with permission from the author.

Mary Dodson Wade, "Buried Christmas Tree." Copyright © 2002 by Mary Dodson Wade. Printed with permission from the author.

Jerry Wermund, "Port O'Connor 9/1/99." Copyright © 2002 by Jerry Wermund. Printed with permission from the author.

David Williams, "Migration Midpoint: What We Can See from Here." Copyright © 2002 by David Williams. Printed with permission from the author.

Raymond E. Williams, "Vacant Lot." Copyright © 2002 by Raymond E. Williams. Printed with permission from the author.

Sylvia B. Williams, "The Singing River." Copyright © 2002 by Sylvia B. Williams. Printed with permission from the author.

Edward O. Wilson, "Alabama Dreaming," excerpted from *Naturalist* (Washington, D.C.: Shearwater Books, 1994), 82–91. Copyright © 1994 by Island Press. Reprinted with permission from Island Press.

Steve Wilson, "The Softshell Turtle." Copyright © 2002 by Steve Wilson. Printed with permission from the author.

Abe Louise Young, "Public School." Copyright © 2002 by Abe Louise Young. Printed with permission from the author.

# About the Editor

Sara St. Antoine grew up in Ann Arbor, Michigan. She holds a bachelor's degree in English from Williams College and a master's degree in environmental studies from the Yale School of Forestry and Environmental Studies. Currently living in Cambridge, Massachusetts, she enjoys walking along the Charles River and seeing black-crowned night herons hunkered in the trees.

## About the Illustrators

Paul Mirocha is a designer and illustrator of books about nature for children and adults. His first book, *Gathering the Desert*, by Gary Paul Nabhan, won the 1985 John Burroughs Medal for natural history. He lives in Tucson, Arizona, with his daughters, Anna and Claire.

Trudy Nicholson is an illustrator of nature with a background in medical and scientific illustration. She received her B.S. in fine arts at Columbia University and has worked as a natural-science illustrator in a variety of scientific fields for many years. She lives in Cabin John, Maryland.

The World As Home, the nonfiction publishing program of Milkweed Editions, is dedicated to exploring our relationship to the natural world. Not espousing any particular environmentalist or political agenda, these books are a forum for distinctive literary writing that not only alerts the reader to vital issues but offers personal testimonies to living harmoniously with other species in urban, rural, and wilderness communities.

Milkweed Editions publishes with the intention of making a humane impact on society, in the belief that literature is a transformative art uniquely able to convey the essential experiences of the human heart and spirit. To that end, Milkweed publishes distinctive voices of literary merit in handsomely designed, visually dynamic books, exploring the ethical, cultural, and esthetic issues that free societies need continually to address. Milkweed Editions is a not-for-profit press.

For more information on other books published by Milkweed Editions for intermediate readers, contact Milkweed at (800) 520-6455 or visit our website (www.milkweed.org).

Books for Middle-Grade Readers
by Milkweed Editions

*Tides* by V. M. Caldwell

*The Ocean Within* by V. M. Caldwell

*The Monkey Thief* by Aileen Kilgore Henderson

*Treasure of Panther Peak* by Aileen Kilgore Henderson

*The Dog with Golden Eyes* by Frances Wilbur

## Milkweed Editions

Founded in 1979, Milkweed Editions is one of the largest independent, nonprofit literary publishers in the United States. Milkweed publishes with the intention of making a humane impact on society, in the belief that great writing can transform the human heart and spirit. Within this mission, Milkweed publishes in four areas: fiction, nonfiction, poetry, and children's literature for middle-grade readers.

## Join Us

Milkweed depends on the generosity of foundations and individuals like you, in addition to the sales of its books. In an increasingly consolidated and bottom-line-driven publishing world, your support allows us to select and publish books on the basis of their literary quality and the depth of their message. Please visit our Web site (www.milkweed.org) or contact us at (800) 520-6455 to learn more about our donor program.

Interior design by Wendy Holdman
The text is typeset in 12/16 point Legacy Book
by Stanton Publication Services, Inc.
Printed on acid-free, recycled 55# Natural Odyssey Hibulk paper
by Friesen Corporation.